HOW TO BE THE BEST SPEAKER IN TOWN

*To all my friends at Platform Professionals, the
National Speakers Association and Toastmasters International*

HOW TO BE THE BEST SPEAKER IN TOWN

Doug Malouf

Business & Professional Publishing

First published 1995
Reprinted 1997
Reprinted 1999
by Business & Professional Publishing
Unit 7/5 Vuko Place, Warriewood NSW 2102

© Dougmal Training Systems 1995

ISBN 1 875680 25 X.

All rights reserved. Apart from any fair dealing for the purpose of study, research or review, as permitted under Australian copyright law, no part of this book may be reproduced by any means without the written permission of the publisher.

Malouf, Doug.
How to be the best speaker in town.

    Bibliography.
    Includes index.
    ISBN 1 875680 25 X.

    1. Public speaking. I. Title.

808.51

Writing consultant:	Margaret McAlister
Chapter contributors:	Craig Griffin
	Rebekah Van den Berg
Illustrations:	Allan Stomann
Index:	Caroline Colton & Associates
Text design:	Kim Webber
Cover design:	Drawing A Living

Printed in Australia by Ligare Pty Ltd

Other books by the author
The Real Estate Sales Survival Kit (now international)
How to be the Best Speaker in Town
How to K.I.S.S. and Keep Your Customers and Kick the Competition
How To Create and Deliver a Dynamic Presentation (now international)
Selling is a Cinch
Switch on Your Magnetic Personality
How To Teach Adults in a Fun and Exciting Way

FOREWORD

Lack of self-confidence is one of the most frequent complaints posed to psychologists. So how does someone overcome lack of self-confidence? By demonstrating a skill and receiving feedback from others that you did an outstanding job! Doug Malouf suggests public speaking as a unique opportunity to improve self-confidence and enhance your career path. Public speaking provides the platform for you to build skills and confidence, and receive quick, direct feedback.

How do you get started? What do you need to learn? Everyone is pressed for time these days, so what are the fastest steps to take in acquiring the skill of public speaking? If you are interested in getting started in a sure-fire, tried and proven manner, this is the book for you. Doug's ability to describe step-by-step measures, one of his hallmark traits, gives you an easy map to success.

As you walk this path to greater word power, notice two things:

* the wonderful gems of wisdom laid at your feet
* the quality role model Doug becomes as he shows you a clear, effortless path to follow—carved from his years of hard work, study and practice.

If you decide to embark on the adventure of public speaking, you could have no better, more knowledgable guide than Doug Malouf.

Join the thousands of professionals Doug has trained in his clear, commonsense approach to acquiring top notch public speaking skills.

Henry Morrow, EdD
Consulting Psychologist

CONTENTS

Foreword		v
Preface		viii
Acknowledgments		x
1	Word power—why bother?	1
2	The great confidence booster	13
3	Nerves and all that jazz	24
4	Different strokes for different folks	37
5	Structuring your speech	53
6	Writing a script	68
7	Knowing what to say—keeping a speech file	78
8	Practising your speech	88
9	Voice power	98
10	Painting mental pictures	109
11	Common problems and practical solutions	118
12	Your Self-Improvement Program	132
Recommended reading		153
Index		155

PREFACE

Everywhere we go we are bombarded by visual stimuli. Flashing signs. Huge billboards. Attention-grabbing colours and shapes. It's obvious to anyone that our society relies heavily on visual cues to both absorb and impart information. But in this Information Age, it pays to remember that we also live, play and work in a society that relies heavily on words as tools—and used skilfully, words can be powerful tools indeed.

It's very easy to get carried away by visual presentations and special effects, but simple, powerful words are more often than not the deciding factor when it comes to making a sale, securing a job or swaying people to your point of view.

You may have purchased this book because, for the first time ever, you have to give a speech. Or you might have a growing awareness that you are not communicating as effectively as you might be. Perhaps you missed out on that promotion you were counting on, or you feel you are not getting through to your co-workers. Or is it simply that, having delivered a number of speeches, you're becoming bored with your communication style?

Whatever prompted you to pick up this book, you'll find plenty of useful advice in its pages. Speaking in public is not a mysterious gift bestowed on the lucky few at birth. It's merely a skill. And what happens when you polish and practise any skill? That's right. It just keeps on getting better. All the outstanding speakers you have heard know this very well. They have practised, rehearsed and refined their communication skills until they make the whole process seem effortless.

I've been in the speaking business more years than I care to remember. I've observed thousands of speakers, and I can tell you that the ones that stand out from the crowd are those who care about communication on every level. They understand that effective speaking is more than just a formula: it's a skill to be practised every day of their lives. They care enough to make sure people understand exactly where they're coming from and what they have to say. They care enough to choose the most appropriate expressions, words and gestures to make their message as effective as possible.

That's powerful speaking.

Preface

Your communication style can be just as powerful. Don't just read this book, shelve it and then go on your merry way wishing you had the time and energy to put it all into practice. Instead, commit to becoming a professional student of public speaking. Go to workshops. Read more books. Above all, speak at every opportunity. Become involved with magnificent organisations like Toastmasters, Apex, View and Rostrum. Join any association that will help you stand up and say what you mean effectively and efficiently.

Finally, become very aware that public speaking is an extension of private speaking. Hone your skills in one area and the benefits flow over to the other. Search for words that motivate, stimulate, amuse or inspire, whether you are communicating with your family or an audience of 200. Strive to make the use of vivid, effective speech second nature. Then you, too, will have at your disposal one of the most powerful tools of the 1990s—Word Power.

Doug Malouf

ACKNOWLEDGMENTS

Everything I do involves a cast of thousands, and I must thank the people around me who have motivated me to write this book.

Margaret McAlister — Writing Consultant and Project Manager
Craig Griffin — Public Speaking Trainer
Rebekah Van den Berg — Voice Trainer
Janice Dawson — Desktop Publishing
Joanna Hughes — Project Co-ordinator
Lyn Chard — Financial Consultant
Allan Stomann — Creative Graphics
Dr Henry Morrow — For his words of wisdom

1

WORD POWER—WHY BOTHER?

Most of us spend a large part of our day talking. We may start with 'We're almost out of cornflakes' at breakfast and finish with 'Well, it's good to get that deal wrapped up' at the end of a working day.

Throughout the day, we use the power of speech to inform, command, question, praise, liaise, impress and berate—in other words, to communicate. To get reactions and results.

The power of speech is something that most of us take for granted unless we lose our voices for some reason. *Then* we realise how inconvenient life would be if we had to communicate solely through sign language or the written word!

The power of speech is not the same as word power. When we talk about the power of speech, we are referring to the ability of people to communicate by a series of sounds and tones made by the larynx, mouth and throat, ably assisted by the lungs. We're talking about how great it is that someone else can receive and understand this series of odd noises, and reconstruct meaning from the code. Speech is a miracle.

Word power is something else again. Word power is being able to use the language to communicate with people and express fine shades of meaning. It's knowing the value of pace, vocal variety, pauses and eye contact to enhance meaning and effectiveness.

Word power is being able to pitch our spiel to different people at different levels—in other words, tailoring the vocabulary and rate of delivery, and structuring the sentences, to give ourselves the best possible chance of having the message received and understood.

Word power is having the confidence to speak to large groups or small. Word power is being comfortable about communicating with others, whether you are in a cosy room or the glare of a spotlight. It's knowing what to say to people at parties, knowing how to draw them out and making it easy for *them* to communicate.

If you can use words powerfully, your self-confidence will soar. Knowing you can express yourself and draw out others, you'll quickly feel at ease in any situation. You'll learn from experience how to 'tune in' to others by listening to their tone of voice and the words they use.

So, as you can see, effective speaking, persistently practised and conscientiously developed, will build your self-confidence in leaps and bounds. You will be someone who knows:

★ when to speak
★ when *not* to speak
★ how to say what has to be said effectively and appropriately
★ how to say it so that people remember.

Imprint these facts on your mind:

★ *Words are a tool*. As such, they may be used well or they may be used badly. To use these tools skilfully, you must *want* to use words well—and you must work on developing your skills like any other artisan.
★ *Language cannot be separated from its uses*. You must learn to use the right type of language for each purpose—to persuade, to inform, to inspire and so on.

★ *Verbal communication is self-expression.* You will always be judged on how you present yourself—your true subject, therefore, is always yourself.

★ *Verbal communication involves other people.* To be a truly effective communicator, you must strive to transmit your intended meaning to other people. This is not as easy as you might think. For example, when I say the word 'cup' to you, you can immediately picture what I mean. But if I use words like integrity, ethics or loyalty, your understanding of these words might be completely different from the meaning I intended to give them.

★ *The speaker's message rarely transmits mere facts.* It reflects their attitudes and values. And the listener, in trying to understand the message, brings their attitudes and values to bear on the words they hear. Thus, the meaning you transmit is always greater than the sum of the meaning of the words you have chosen to use.

★ *Effective speakers engage the emotions of their listeners.* A memorable speech does more than just transmit facts. The really effective speaker knows that they have to engage both the emotions and the intellects of their listeners.

★ *Effective speaking is a way of satisfying our needs.* Once we are well-fed, adequately clothed and sheltered, and reasonably secure, we will seek to satisfy our 'higher' needs—things like success, prestige and the approval of others. The ability to speak effectively will bring you closer to the satisfaction of your personal wants and needs. In short, if you can use words that not only say what you mean but that also convince your audience that you mean what you say, you will be much better equipped to realise your potential as a human being.

If you become confident in your ability to express yourself in any situation—social, business or personal—then you are more likely to be successful in all your relationships.

Once you understand these basic facts about communication, you can begin to work at improving your communication skills. Take comfort in the fact that all effective speakers have to start by learning the basics.

MAKING A START

These days, I speak regularly at many overseas functions, and have won awards for communication—but I wasn't born knowing how to speak in public. When I share with you what my first speaking experience was like, you'll see that I had a long, long way to go before I arrived where I am today.

In 1961 I was invited to join the Canowindra Apex Club, part of an international organisation that aims at providing community service and at developing the ideals of good citizenship in the young men who form its membership.

Soon after my membership was formally accepted I was advised that each Apex Club in the district held a public speaking contest. Each club winner then competed at district level. The winner of the district competition went on to zone level, and finally the zone champion went on to compete in the Australian grand final.

Now when the time came to run our internal club competition, no one bothered to listen to each club member speaking. Instead, we held the traditional Aussie raffle. All the names went into the hat and the winner (or the loser, depending on the way you look at it) was drawn. This lucky fellow was to represent our club at the next level of competition at Eugowra.

I was young, green and very naive. Little did I realise that my name was on all of the 26 cards that went into the hat. Guess who was selected? I prepared a magnificent speech entitled 'We Are Digging Our Graves With Our Mouths' which put forward the theory that junk food is slowly destroying our digestive systems. It consisted of seven foolscap pages of double-spaced script. And I had it word perfect.

Word Power—Why Bother?

The big day arrived: a hot Saturday afternoon. The contest was held in the School of Arts building—a huge corrugated iron shed with a stage more than 1 metre from ground level, two doors at the front and one at the back, and very few windows.

I was speaker No. 3. By the time my name was called, there I was hanging on to my seven pages like grim death. I walked out on to the stage and faced the audience: 200 eyes staring at me; 200 ears waiting for my words of wisdom. I neatly arranged my speech on the lectern provided and began:

Ladies and Gentlemen...

At that precise moment someone opened the back door of the School of Arts hall, and the next thing I remember is seeing my wonderful seven-page speech flying out into the crowd in all directions like seven magnificent birds. The next two important words to come from me were: 'Thank you.'

So ended my brilliant career as a public speaker. The shame of it! How could I face my friends at the next club meeting?

I should have known that good friends are always supportive in natural personal disasters. At the next club meeting everyone kept saying: 'That was a great effort!'

Quite bewildered, I asked the club president what was going on. He told me that my effort was good compared to last year's speaker. He hadn't turned up.

Despite this disastrous beginning, I decided I was going to push myself through my own fear. I thought: 'If other people can stand up and speak so everyone listens, so can I!' So I embarked on a self-improvement program.

I read plenty of books. I asked the advice of better speakers at the club. I started to enter (without the raffle) various public speaking contests and debating competitions.

Now, after years of successful speaking engagements, business meetings and running classes on effective speaking for others, I can tell you this:

> *Effective speaking is a personal affair. You can learn from others, but in the end you can't use anybody else's words or methods. You must develop your own speaking style—it comes out of* **who you are**: *your interests, attitudes and values.*

When you think style, think AVIS:

Your	**A**ttitudes
	Values
	Interests
equal your	**S**tyle

SPEAKING 'THEIR' LANGUAGE

Your skill in public speaking will grow out of your skill at communication at *all levels*, with all types of people. Talented communicators adapt their style and vocabulary to their audience, whether that audience consists of one person or a thousand.

If your words are pitched at a level too high or too low for your audience, two things will result: one, you will not communicate your meaning effectively, and, two, you will run the risk of your audience switching off to you permanently.

A friend of mine named Dan had an experience that graphically illustrates the importance of being a good communicator. On the day he came to see me he had been off work for three weeks, and had spent most of those three weeks in hospital, having test after test. I could see he was pretty fed up with the world.

'As it happens, the condition I've got can be controlled with drugs and diet,' he told me, sounding frustrated. 'But it's not the illness getting me down so much as the specialist. The more I try to find out about the disease the more he clams up—or comes out with all this medical jargon that means absolutely nothing to me. All I want to know is what to expect! You know, the symptoms, how long I'll need treatment, what will happen to me in hospital...but do you think I can get a straight answer?'

'Maybe he doesn't like to commit himself in case the disease takes a different tack,' I suggested.

He snorted. 'It's not that, Doug. Even if he said, "Look, in the last 20 cases I've seen, this can happen or this can happen or this can happen, we can't be sure,"—that would be okay. I don't expect the man to be a magician. He just doesn't seem to have a clue about how to talk to his patients.'

There wouldn't be a single one of us who hasn't had an experience like Dan's. Your 'expert' who can't or won't tell you what you want to know could be in the field of computers, business, literature, law or countless other professions. You'll come across people who can't communicate everywhere.

We feel irritated if people assume we're too stupid to understand what they're saying, but it's just as frustrating if they leave us floundering in a sea of jargon. I bet you can remember some occasion when you've been caught by someone who peppers the conversation with seldom-used words. I don't know about you, but my reaction (and, I suspect, that of most people) is one of annoyance and frustration. What's more, I immediately tune out.

How to be the Best Speaker in Town

Powerful speakers have the ability to fine-tune their speech to a specific audience. You show consideration for the listener if you speak in 'their' language. Listen for not only the pace of their communication, but also for the type of vocabulary they use, and whether they use short or long sentences. They'll feel more comfortable talking with you if you adapt your style to one similar to theirs.

When you see someone receiving your message, understanding it and perhaps acting on it, you know you're being effective. Up goes your self-esteem—and up go your chances of putting across a positive self-image.

Examine the pattern of communication shown in the illustration below:

There is no interaction in this situation. The speaker is talking at his audience. There are no positive responses.

Now let's change the picture:

In this case, the speaker is receiving and taking notice of the reactions of his audience. What a difference!

Analyse your daily conversation and communication with other people. If you have a hard time keeping their attention, the chances are that you are either sending very negative messages, or making a series of egocentric statements.

When you're speaking, it sometimes helps to visualise a flow of energy being transmitted between you and the listener. (This works equally well for one-on-one or large audiences.) If it helps, picture two pipelines: one from them to you, the other from you to them.

You transmit energy to your listeners via stimulating thoughts and interesting anecdotes. You take energy from them if you have them struggling to understand because of obscure terminology, too much information or a monotonous tone (or endless stories about yourself). Make it a practice to read the energy level and react accordingly—by cutting out some information, stopping to tell a story to illustrate your point, changing to a chattier style, or simply stopping to listen and draw out the other person.

Communicating effectively involves a change in attitude towards yourself, other people and the language you use.

Think before you speak!

THE FIRST STEP: THE FIVE MINUTE TEST

Here's a quick test you can take to analyse your ability to communicate in a way that interests others. You will need:

* a pen
* a piece of paper
* some creative thinking
* five minutes of your time (not one or three minutes—five minutes).

Now that you've gathered your equipment together write a brief talk on the subject that you know most about. Yourself! Give yourself just five minutes to do it—and *think before you write*. Do it now, before you read any further.

When you have finished, read your story. Does it go something like this?

My name is Elizabeth Smith, and I live at 10 Smith Street, Dullsville. I am married to Alan and we have three children. My occupation is bank teller, and I have been with the bank for the past 15 years…

Need we continue? If your story reads like that, imagine what it would do to an audience if you were delivering it as a speech in a public speaking competition! There is only one word for this story: *boring*.

On the other hand, if you were to come out of the five minute test with flying colours, your story would read something like this:

Over the past 15 years, I have been doing what everybody in this room would like to do—counting money. Mind you, it's not my own, but my occupation is both interesting and exciting because I am involved with people from all walks of life. **Have you guessed yet? I'm a bank teller.**

Anyone can see the two presentations vary a great deal. Yet the difference lies only in the words that have been used. One version is so standard that it's boring. The other is capable of holding the interest of the listeners because it takes their points of view into account. They want to listen to a story—not a boring recount.

It doesn't really matter whether you passed or failed the five minute test. You are, after all, a beginner. There's a lot of learning ahead of you—if you already knew everything there is to know about effective speaking you wouldn't need this book.

PERSISTENCE PAYS

If you pick up any book on self-improvement you will find that the most important quality you need is *self-confidence*. And self-confidence comes, in part, from developing effective communication skills.

There is no magic formula that, when mixed, brewed and swallowed, will turn you into an instant speaker. There is just one basic requirement: that you simply want to improve. That determination, and a steady program to build up your skills, will get you to where you want to go.

As you improve, force yourself to seek out experiences and look for challenges. Sure, there will be ups and downs. I've been teaching and experiencing public speaking for 25 years now—and I *still* suffer from nerves.

These days I criss-cross the world, seeing and talking with the best. Most of these speakers still suffer from nerves. They tell me, too, that they have done countless boring speeches to get ready for the big event, and they are adamant about one thing: *persistence pays*. There's no getting away from it: personal effort plays a massive part in your personal development.

I'm very much aware that some of my speeches are better than others. But the underlying element of self-confidence remains, regardless of the success or failure of actual performances.

Seeking out new public speaking experiences and meeting new challenges provide the only real means of improving your effectiveness as a speaker. The hard work involved will strengthen and build your character.

Increasing your word power is hard work, and potentially embarrassing, but the rewards are tremendous. Make the effort, and your entire personality will change.

You will find yourself at ease in any social situation. And people will watch you speak and think, 'If only I could speak like that...'

IN SUMMARY...

- ✶ Most people are physically capable of speaking, but powerful communication skills must be learned.
- ✶ The ability to speak effectively builds your self-confidence. If you become confident in your ability to express yourself, you are more likely to be successful socially, personally and professionally.
- ✶ Words are a tool. You can use this tool skilfully or badly.
- ✶ There is a right kind of language for each purpose.
- ✶ Effective speakers engage the emotions of their listeners.
- ✶ Effective speaking is a personal affair. You can learn from others, but in the end you must develop your own speaking style.

STYLE = Attitude + Values + Interests

- ★ You transmit energy to your listeners via stimulating thoughts and interesting anecdotes. You take energy from them by boring or confusing them.
- ★ There is no magic formula to turn you into a gifted speaker. Everyone follows the same path: learn, practise, improve.
- ★ Keep looking for new challenges.

2

THE GREAT CONFIDENCE BOOSTER

Craig Griffin is one of the accredited presenters for Dougmal Training Systems International. He works with over 5000 people every year, sharing his dynamic ideas on public speaking. I have invited him to share his perceptions of what public speaking is all about, and to tell us what confidence in public speaking has done for him.

Some time ago, an old work colleague of mine came over to me just after I'd finished speaking at a seminar. In our previous work roles, he had watched me bumble my way through quite a few presentations, so it gave me a real lift when he said: 'Congratulations! Great presentation. I can't believe the difference since the last time I heard you speak. What've you been doing, taking lessons?'

'Thanks,' I said. 'Not lessons, exactly. I started to move forward once I realised that speaking in public is nothing more than a skill.' I grinned. 'And like any other skill, it improves with practice. So I started practising.'

What I was passing on to my colleague was an insight that I gained after listening to and talking with Doug Malouf. I realised that although most of us are born with the inherent ability to use language, *no one* comes into this world with a label saying 'talented speaker'. No one is tagged 'hopeless', either. *Anyone* can improve. Anyone can build up their skills. All it takes is determination, confidence and *practice*.

Once I realised this, I set about overcoming my fear of public speaking. And judging from my friend's comments and further advice, I was on the right track—although I had a long way to go before I could make a living from speaking.

My friend also told me a story about his father that really cemented my beliefs about how important it is for anyone to master the skills of public speaking. Apparently his father, a tradesman with little formal education, took himself off at the age of about 40 to attend a public speaking course.

He expected his new-found skills to be of some benefit, but even he was stunned by the extent to which his business grew after he started using what he'd learnt. He attributes that business growth directly to the development of advanced communication skills, and the accompanying increase in his self-confidence.

I haven't seen my friend since that seminar, but his parting words stay with me. He said, 'Isn't it amazing how some of the most intelligent people can be so inadequate as speakers, yet your average Joe can sound like a guru if he just knows how to put himself across in public.'

I guess this comment summarises my real belief about achieving results. The people who achieve the best results in their careers are those with superior communication skills. And the most powerful form of communication is undoubtedly the ability to speak before a crowd.

You don't have to look too far to find historical evidence. The great Winston Churchill, a stutterer as a child, employed his own personal style to unite and motivate thousands and thousands of people. An orator such as Martin Luther King could emotionally move huge crowds with an address. Betty Friedan and Germaine Greer, through their written and spoken words, encouraged millions of women to think more deeply about their roles.

The truth of the matter is that you don't need to be a Martin Luther King or a Winston Churchill, or a Germaine Greer, to reap the benefits of fine-tuning your public speaking skills. I regularly conduct seminars to help people overcome their fear of public speaking, and I never get tired of seeing the growth people experience when they develop their skills.

EXACTLY WHAT WILL PUBLIC SPEAKING DO FOR YOU?

As I sat down to write this chapter, I thought more deeply about why the development of public speaking skills has such an amazing effect on self-confidence generally. My thoughts led me to a recent experience of my own that required tremendous self-confidence.

A while back, I paid a great deal of money to learn to walk across red hot rocks. Some of you will no doubt be raising your eyebrows and thinking that to pay good money to walk across hot rocks I must have rocks in the head. However, the presenter used the fire walk as a metaphor for overcoming fear. And what is the number one fear in the Western world? That's right: public speaking. No wonder, then, that mastery of public speaking skills does so much to boost people's self-confidence.

What an incredibly powerful tool.

Invariably, good speakers are highly regarded in our culture. We all admire people who are able to speak with conviction and passion. If you spend a moment thinking about some well-known sporting personalities young people look up to, you will realise that those heroes are not necessarily the number one players in their sports. Often, they are simply the best communicators. And those good communicators find that their sporting careers extend well past the 'use by' date of their bodies which are no longer at match-winning fitness.

They move on to become commentators, speakers and consultants. They build, run and promote their own businesses. They present themselves with confidence at business meetings and negotiations.

Many of us don't realise how significantly our careers may be affected by our performance in meetings. We are tempted sometimes to take a back seat—to let the others argue and make decisions. Maybe we don't have a choice about attending, but no one can make us take an active role, right?

Right. But if you don't speak up, no one can be blamed for overlooking you when it comes to appointing people for more important tasks, either. Meetings are an ideal opportunity to influence others and to display your ability to lead, organise, inform and motivate. You can impress the boss. You can impress colleagues. You can impress clients. In short, the employment of your speaking skills in meetings can be a career enhancing strategy.

You don't have to look far to find successful business professionals who have employed this strategy. When it comes to gardening I'm sure that Don Burke is no Sir Joseph Banks, yet his speaking and presentation skills have accelerated his career to the point where he is a household name. Don would probably be the first to admit that there are gardeners with more knowledge and more qualifications than he has. Some of them may even work behind the scenes on 'Burke's Backyard'. But who is the 'gardening guru'? Don Burke, the gardener with the laid back charm, the whimsical sense of humour. The gardener with the ability to communicate with you, his audience, in a way that makes you feel you are having a chat with a knowledgable friend.

And why do people turn to Dr Rosie King to find out information on subjects from puberty to piles, from rubella to relationships? Not because she has the best qualifications in her field. Because she is a presenter with pizzazz.

All in all, it's pretty evident that mastery of public speaking skills will do wonders for your career. But why is public speaking such a powerful self-development tool? There are two reasons:

★ the mastery of public speaking skills requires you to grow
★ the results are immediately tangible.

Unlike many of the other personal development strategies we undertake, in which results are long-term and sometimes intangible, within a very short time we can see results for our efforts—and so can others.

OVERCOMING A POOR SELF-IMAGE

The following activity is one that I regularly use with participants of my seminars to help people develop their public speaking skills. It's a simple, effective way of changing your own mindset about public speaking. Try it. Use it regularly, and see the difference it makes.

HOW DO YOU SEE YOURSELF?

Hello Me!

Get comfortable, and close your eyes for a moment. Let your mind focus on someone you respect as a presenter or public speaker…

As you picture this person, tune in to the size of the image. How do you picture this person standing? As a strong, bright image? Up close to you? Or distant and faded? Are they in black and white, or full colour? What is this person's posture like?

Now listen as this person begins to speak. How strong is their voice? Do they sound meek and squeaky, or strong and resonant? When you 'hear' them speak, what kind of a feeling do they impart?

Now think back to a time when you were called upon to speak in front of a group. What is *this* image like? Are you strong and bright, or distant and faded? Is the picture coloured, or black and white? How is your posture? How is your voice? What kind of feelings arise as you picture yourself speaking?

During this activity, did you notice any difference between the way that you represent yourself and the way you represented the other speaker in your mind?

Typically, people represent their own image quite differently from the way they represent a respected speaker.

By changing the way we represent our own images, we can dramatically improve our self-confidence. So let's see what we can do about it right now. It's time to reconfigure your own mind.

RECONFIGURING YOUR MIND

Bring back that image of the person you respect as a speaker and embed it firmly in your mind. Now go back to the image you have of yourself. Look carefully at both, and notice the differences.

Focus again on the image of the respected speaker or presenter. This time examine *exactly* how you represent this person. Now switch back to the image of yourself and set to work. Gradually change your own image until it reflects the same brightness, confidence and clarity as that of the speaker you admire.

How does it look? How does it sound? What do you feel?

The Great Confidence Booster

Simply by doing this activity a number of times, we can reconfigure the mental image we have of ourselves as speakers. Through practice, we can reduce pre-speech nerves and anxiety. By reducing this anxiety, we improve both our preparation and our delivery.

Remember: speaking is a skill that needs practice to be perfect.

Whenever I run the above activity, I never fail to find a number of people who represent themselves in a very different light from the way they represent someone they respect as a speaker. Their self-image is very poor.

The first step in overcoming poor self-image is *awareness*.

Quite often, we are not aware of what we are doing to ourselves. Once we realise that we are, in effect, sabotaging our own success, we can begin to change things. The development of confidence is all about being patient. You will notice some impact the first time you try this activity, but those who really reap the rewards are those who have patience. Those who know that, with persistence, they will improve.

How easy is it to reconfigure your mind and build confidence in public speaking? To develop these skills to the stage where you are having an impact and making a difference?

It would be stretching the truth if I told you that becoming a great public speaker is easy. Most learning brings with it some degree of discomfort. My dear mother, Shirley Griffin, always told me that nothing worthwhile comes easily. Fortunately, public speaking doesn't have to be a painful process. It can even be fun. But it will mean that you have to take a few steps outside your comfort zone.

When you move outside your comfort zone, you can take it as a sign that you're learning something. Unfortunately, most people will do anything to avoid discomfort. They hold themselves back. They grab for the safety of what is familiar rather than taking the risks associated with moving, growing and learning.

TRUST IS A MUST

There are many cultural reasons for fear of public speaking. It may be triggered by old patterns from our childhood—for example, 'Speak when you're spoken to!' Women, particularly, may be intimidated by childhood conditioning that builds a psychological resistance to speaking out and 'being noticed'.

As we move to the new millennium, in an economy driven more by information and knowledge rather than making and moving things, speaking only when spoken to may not be the most effective career enhancing strategy available. In fact, it is estimated that by the year 2000 a large percentage of today's jobs will not even exist. Furthermore, people entering the workforce today can expect to retrain up to four times. In this Information Age, those who can access and share information and knowledge will find themselves well on the way to success. This transformation is already evident in the seminar and meeting business.

One of the sure-fire ways to improve your public speaking skills is to *practise, rehearse and drill*. All too often, people seek me out to complain that the more practice they do the worse their speech delivery seems to become. These people are all labouring under the same misconception: practice and rehearsal equals memorisation.

Nothing could be further from the truth.

Recently, a good friend of mine was called upon to speak at a wedding. Never one to do anything by halves, he wrote, practised and rehearsed a speech that he felt would be a sure-fire winner. A careful man, he wrote out his speech on cue cards cut to fit exactly in the palm of his hand. Just before the wedding he tucked the cards neatly inside his wife's handbag.

Well, I bet you can guess what's coming next. Yes, his wife made a last minute decision to take the brown handbag, not the black one. My friend didn't discover the blunder until he went to his wife to get his cue cards for a last-minute skim over the content in the men's room.

Disaster. Those meticulously prepared cue cards were a two-hour drive from the ceremony. A major panic attack followed: all my friend could think about was how he would *never* be able to remember the speech. Predictably, when he was called upon to speak, he went blank. Instead of relaxing and trusting that his mind would provide him with the key points, he tried to grind it out word for word. Halfway through, he got totally lost. Barely able to remember his *own* name, he got the bride's name wrong. Unfortunately he substituted the name of a previous girlfriend. For a moment you could have heard a pin drop, then the sniggers started.

At the end of this horrendous ordeal, my friend sought me out for some feedback (and probably some reassurance that this hadn't really been the Wedding From Hell). I said, as any friend would, 'Uh—well done, mate.'

He looked at me and said flatly, 'You must be joking. I was appalling.'

I tried to be reassuring. (In hindsight, I think it probably sounded patronising instead.) 'Well,' I said, 'you did what you could.'

The Great Confidence Booster

He shook his head ruefully. 'I learnt three things today. One, never trust your wife with important documents. Two, if you run into trouble in the middle of a speech only ever talk about yourself. And three—I'll never prepare another speech!'

It was a classic defensive reaction. But what was the real lesson in this scenario? After my friend's debacle, I decided to do some research into how the mind works. He wasn't, after all, the first example I'd seen of the mind shutting up shop in times of stress. What could I learn from this to help other beginning speakers?

The material I found to be of the most use concerned left brain/right brain functions. The brain, it seems, consists of two hemispheres: the left and the right. Each side of the brain has a different function. The left side of the brain likes to deal with numbers, order, logic and sequence. If you are thinking about 'what comes next' in a speech, you are using the left side of the brain.

If you are desperately trying to recall a speech word for word, and you forget a word and disrupt the sequence, your brain begins to panic. It moves straight into left brain mode. In effect, this is much like being a learner driver wondering how to get out of first gear. You are so busy trying to think of what comes next it becomes impossible to deliver effectively. Far better to call on the right brain.

The right side of the brain deals with colour, patterns, flow and movement. These are the characteristics of a well-delivered presentation.

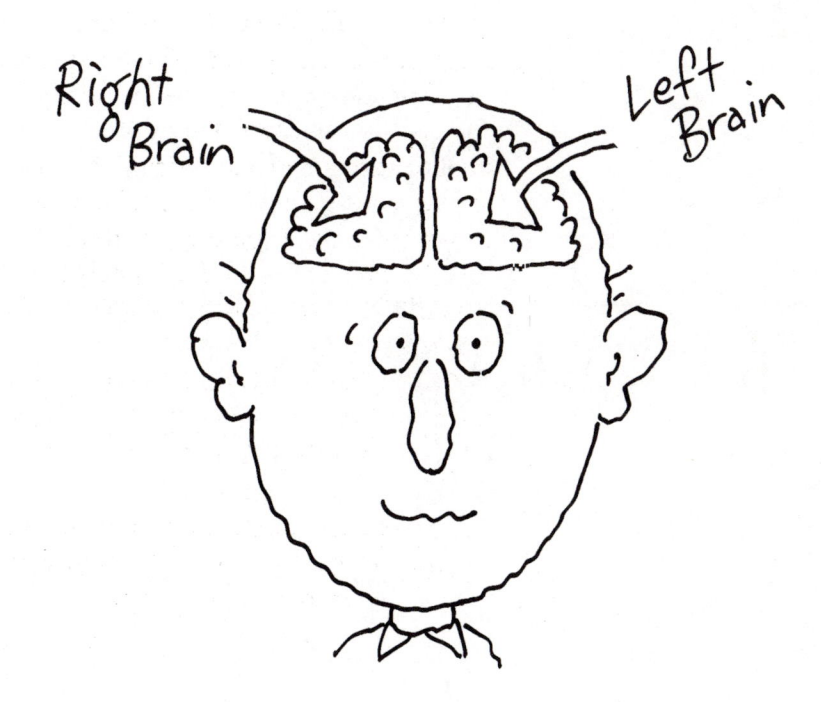

So how do you access the right brain during a presentation? The answer's simple. (Maybe not what you want to hear, but definitely simple.) You simply need to *prepare and practise* so that your brain creates a net of neurones to capture the speech. Your mind becomes convinced that you have indeed trapped all the facts necessary to make a smooth delivery. That's the way to set up the conditions necessary to move easily into a 'right brain' presentation.

A friend of mine who plays golf professionally has a wonderful, memorable quote about this right brain mode:

Loose as a Goose—Trust is a Must.

It says it all. I've adopted it to use for public speaking. So prepare your speech well, but don't attempt to memorise it. If you freeze, it's a recipe for disaster.

Recently, I helped a colleague (who happens to be a professional speaker) to develop an audio tape series. Part of the series was to be taped in front of a live audience. My colleague was a bit worried. She knew that audio productions are an unforgiving media. She carefully developed a script and attempted a word perfect rendition in front of a live audience.

Obviously I wouldn't be telling you this story if things had worked out. About three minutes into the presentation she missed a word. Her brain said: *start again*. (After all, that's what she did in practice.) It was a bit like going back to the start of a CD track to run through a certain part again.

Predictably, she became stuck in low gear. The vitality was missing from her presentation until she moved on to a less scripted part of the presentation that involved the audience. Then her right brain kicked in, and the whole delivery picked up momentum. She learnt a lot about trusting the right side of her brain that day.

IN SUMMARY...

The main things I've learnt about public speaking can be summarised in a few, easily remembered points:

★ Being an effective public speaker will boost your self-confidence and enhance your career prospects.
★ Public speaking is a skill.

- ★ Any skill improves with practice.
- ★ Know the *essence* of your message inside out and back to front and you won't have to memorise it.
- ★ Let your left brain prepare and plan your speech, but trust your right brain to take over to deliver it.

3

NERVES AND ALL THAT JAZZ

Okay, you're ready to bite the bullet and start working on being an effective public speaker. There's just one small problem...you break out in a cold sweat at the very thought. ('Me? Standing in front of a group of people? Making a speech? No. I don't think I can...')

I'd be leading you down the garden path if I tried to tell you that you'll find giving a speech just as easy as chatting over the fence with your neighbour, or discussing work practices with your colleagues. (Although one day you might think just that—who knows?)

It has been said that speaking in public is like sex: we are anxious before, excited during, and as soon as it's over we think: 'You know, I could do that again!'

Nerves and all that Jazz

The trouble is, as far as public speaking is concerned, most people never get to the stage of thinking 'I could do that again' for the very good reason that they're too scared to give it a go in the first place. The very thought of standing up in front of an audience, looking out at that sea of faces, turns people into piteous quivering lumps. Their throats become dry. Their hands grow clammy. Death seems a welcome release.

Too melodramatic? Not a bit of it. A survey done some years ago showed that some people put 'speaking in public' as the number one fear on a list that included fear of spiders, fear of heights and fear of death. So it's official—there are those among us who would rather die than speak!

So what do you do if you shake at the thought of speaking in public, but find yourself in a situation where you can no longer avoid it?

Simply by approaching public speaking systematically, you'll realise that writing and delivering a speech is a straightforward process. You don't have to be a magician. You don't have to be a 'born speaker', either. If you take it step by step, you'll end up with a good, effective presentation.

It's natural for you to have a few worries, though—the same fears that everyone has when they make their first speech. Most of your anxiety is probably based on those old myths about speaking, such as:

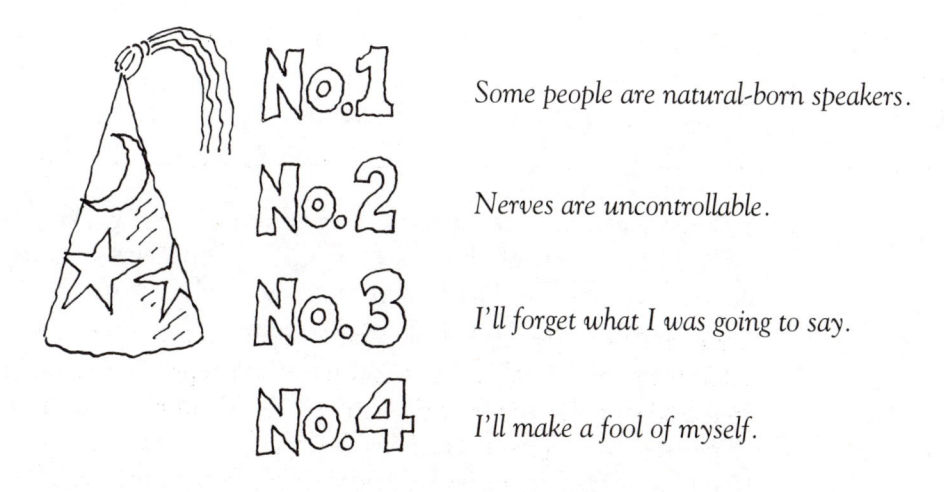

No. 1 — Some people are natural-born speakers.

No. 2 — Nerves are uncontrollable.

No. 3 — I'll forget what I was going to say.

No. 4 — I'll make a fool of myself.

These fears are like big beady-eyed vultures flapping around in your thoughts, ready to dive down and tear your self-confidence to shreds. So let's shoot them down before they can do any damage!

MYTH NO. 1: THE NATURAL SPEAKER SYNDROME

You probably already know from being in the audience yourself over the years that the most popular speakers are those who speak in a relaxed, conversational manner. The most unpopular are those who read from a long written speech and act as if they don't even know they have an audience of live human beings out there.

But if you're thinking that only 'natural-born' speakers sound relaxed and confident when they speak, think again. Those speakers who sound as though they arrived in this world with a microphone in their hands are good because they practise. Again and again and again. And because they never stop learning.

From the moment we are born, slapped on the bottom and become a part of this big wide world, we become victims of our environment. Psychiatrists tell us that the fears of parents often become the fears of their children. For example, if your parents were afraid of dogs, it is not likely that you would have had much contact with dogs as a child. It would also be quite likely that you would be nervous about dogs yourself. What does this have to do with effective speaking?

If your parents were not involved in public affairs, if they never engaged in public speaking, or if they didn't encourage you to take part in school debates, then your chances of development as a public speaker would be much less than those of a person whose parents had been experienced speakers and encouraged their children to develop the same skills.

Therefore when we say that a person is a natural speaker, we might simply be recognising that they are seasoned speakers who have been encouraged to engage in different types of public speaking. They have gained a rich background of speaking experiences. *It's all a matter of learning*. And we can't learn skills unless someone provides the incentive and opportunity to practise them.

Some high schools these days actively encourage all forms of public speaking. Given these opportunities, students who want to can quickly learn to become effective speakers. None of them is a 'natural speaker'—although some might have absorbed the right techniques because members of their families speak in public. The ability to speak effectively develops out of the experiences provided by the school.

History has produced many famous individuals, some with tremendous physical handicaps, who have developed the art of successful speaking, simply because they have burnt three magic words into their minds:

I want to.

Wanting to has been their personal strength.

The decision to improve your public speaking skills is a personal choice. Don't waste time blaming your parents or your environment for your deficiencies. If you want to, you can improve.

There are plenty of professional groups and bodies that will help you to develop and improve your methods of communication if you provide the motivation. In this country, you can improve at anything, if you want to.

MYTH NO. 2: NERVES ARE UNCONTROLLABLE

Imagine your mind to be like those radio transmitters that can't do two things at once. They can either receive or transmit. Just what they transmit depends on you. If you are preoccupied with your nervous tension, then nervous impulses take the place of the transmitting impulses. Is that the message you want to get across?

I have seen a person stand up to speak to a group of people without being able to produce a single word. Their anxiety was so great it totally blocked their ability to speak.

What you need to remember is this:

You will never lose your nervous tension in any social performance.

Believe me when I say: you wouldn't want to. It's part of your performance. Ask any professional actor or musician. They will tell you that, even after years of rehearsals and performances, they still need the stimulation of their nervous reactions to help them perform at maximum efficiency. So instead of trying to lose your nervousness and fears, simply learn to control them and make them work for you.

To combat nervous tension, you must make your nervous system your slave, not your master. To do this you must learn how to relax. Relaxation is a most important part of developing effective communication skills.

Relaxation: your mind is the power source.

If you have your mind under control, you will be under control. Here are some techniques I use, which work every time.

Auto-suggestion

Before you speak in public, visualise the scene—the room, the chairs and the platform. Then imagine your audience gradually filing in, filling the rows of seats. When the room is full, envisage the chairperson making a few introductory comments, then calling upon you to speak.

Picture yourself slowly walking to the lectern and then standing there, looking at the crowd. You are nervous, but controlled. You know your material. You know the audience will want to hear what you have to say. You smile at them, and confidently begin your speech.

If you have put enough detail into this imaginary situation, you should actually feel the natural anxiety attached to the real situation. And if you have controlled yourself in the imaginary situation you are 60 per cent of the way home! This is exactly the technique used by many of our most talented athletes before a game or a competition. It works for them, and it will work for you.

Deep breathing

Another effective way to develop self-control in the public speaking situation is through controlled *deep breathing*. Inhale, and count slowly to four. *Think* of the numbers. Actually *see* them in your imagination— 1, 2, 3, 4. Then exhale slowly thinking:

I am in control.

This technique of deep breathing, counting and learning to pause will give you a tremendous feeling of platform control. And if you always follow this procedure of *deep breathing* followed by *slow counting* when you are getting ready for a speaking engagement, the routine will become a habit. It will become a subconscious part of your behaviour that will help you to be in full control of yourself when speaking in public.

So remember:

* Create the speaking situation in your mind before the event so that you can feel and control the tension created by it.
* Practise deep breathing and slow counting as a means of controlling your nerves in the real situation.

Used frequently, these techniques will increase your confidence on the public speaking platform. In time, they will become second nature. You will get up to speak feeling as though you are master of the situation. The subconscious habits you have developed will lead to conscious self-control and confidence.

Try printing the following nerve-busters on a small card to keep in your pocket. If you're feeling nervous before a presentation, pull it out and go through the three steps on the card.

NERVE-BUSTERS

Feeling nervous? Try this:

1. Visualise yourself standing confidently, giving your speech to a responsive, involved audience.
2. Use the deep breathing technique:
   — Inhale and count slowly: 1, 2, 3, 4.
   — Exhale slowly while thinking: *I am in control.*
3. Memorise your opening lines and deliver them with a smile.

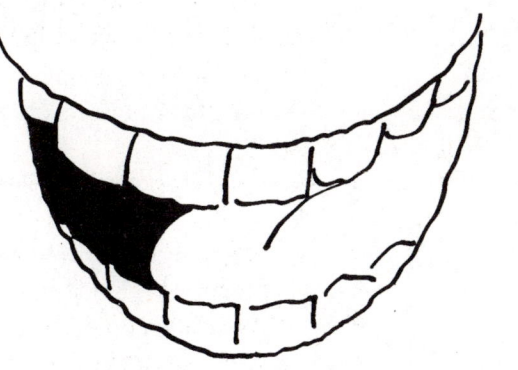

Another method of reducing your nerves is to become an expert on your subject. Read and read about your topic. Jot down important points. Explain your subject matter to anyone who will listen (especially a 12-year-old—they'll soon cut you down if you're obscure or boring). Be sure in your own mind that you can speak confidently on any aspect of your subject.

MYTH NO. 3: I'LL FORGET THE SPEECH

The Toastmasters organisation teaches the principle:

All speakers have butterflies. Good speakers teach them to fly in formation.

The key is learning how to control your nerves, and you now know how to do that. Using notes will ensure that you feel more confident. As you become more practised, you will cheerfully do away with your notes—but while you're learning, if you feel more secure holding notes—then do so.

It is easy to set yourself up to forget. One way of doing this is to try to be word perfect. (That was the trouble with *my* very first public speaking performance. I *was* word perfect. So when one word was forgotten, my pattern of thought was disrupted and my whole speech went out the window!) Remember:

★ **DON'T** psych yourself up to forget.
★ **DON'T** try to be word perfect.

Professional actors and television stars use cue cards, so why shouldn't you? But learn from my experience with loose sheets of paper. Card-size, hand-held notes won't blow away if someone opens a door!

Used correctly, neat, compact notes will help you to feel confident and relaxed, so that you can think and speak clearly. *Notes are better than a script*, for the simple reason that using a script means that you tend to lose spontaneity.

(Having said that, I'll now tell you that in Chapter 6 you will find advice on preparing a script. Now, if I've just said that notes are better than a script, why would I bother incorporating such a chapter? Quite simply, that chapter on scripts is in this book because I'm a realist. I know that some people will refuse to get up there in front of an audience without a fully written-out speech, and that's that. No matter what I or anyone else says! So if that's going to happen, I figure that at least you should know how to write a script so that it's easy to read from and so your words sound natural.)

MYTH NO. 4: I'LL MAKE A FOOL OF MYSELF

It just isn't sensible for an inexperienced speaker to prepare and present a 20 minute speech to a group of 30 or more people. So if you are a newcomer to public speaking, tread slowly. From my experience, the people who do cause themselves embarrassment are those who are brash, careless and over-confident.

The early speeches are the most difficult because you have to think of so many things. If you can, plan a first performance of no more than three or four minutes in front of a small group. Build up slowly to longer speeches and bigger audiences, always learning from your last experience.

Early in your career as a communicator, *forget* quantity. Go straight for short, high quality speeches and you will be much less likely to find yourself in an embarrassing situation. And always *remain natural*.

Mind Power

I've talked a lot about the role of the mind in visualising public speaking situations and dispelling nerves, but a participant in one of my public speaking courses brought it home to me quite dramatically.

This young man was there, like a lot of others, because his work required him to stand up and give presentations and he thought the course would give him a lot more personal confidence.

He was also blind, and so I wrongly assumed he wouldn't have the same fears as most of the others since he couldn't actually see the audience. Because he didn't have to look at all those faces, I treated his fear a bit lightly. 'You'll be right,' I said. 'You won't have to worry about who is or isn't in the room or whether they're looking at you.' I soon discovered my mistake.

It made no difference that he couldn't see the audience. Every time he stood up, his brain was *telling* him there was an audience there, so he worried as much as anybody about the impact he was having on them. His main problem was that he had no way of getting feedback about how he was doing. He was *listening* so hard to get some sort of idea of how he was doing, he was forgetting his words. His stance and gestures were also a little awkward.

We asked him to embark on a heavy six-week program of *standing* and talking—which it had never occurred to him to do, since he used to sit to practise. He gained a lot of confidence once he stood and started using his hands, and even moving around the room in a confined area. After the six weeks had elapsed, he was speaking like a trouper.

This experience highlighted for me the fact that 99 per cent of a person's fears are subconscious, and if they can simulate the experience in their minds, they can overcome a lot of that nervous tension. It's the fear of new experiences that makes people freeze, break out in a sweat, or forget how to speak.

I had to remind myself of this all over again when I started something new for me: making a video. It was a nerve-wracking experience. Instead of talking to a thousand people, I was talking to one—the camera technician. I had to convince myself that all those people were still out there—I simply had to reach them through the eye of a camera.

So I stuck a picture of a camera on the wall, and a set of eyes, which I pretended was the audience. I did a lot of simulated events, to get me relaxed in front of the camera.

Let me admit here and now that, like everybody else, I *hate* having to practise. I feel self-conscious, and it's time-consuming. I try to put it off. Suddenly there are a hundred and one other things I 'should' be doing...I'm sure you're familiar with the scene!

But when it's time to run through the procedure again, I can see a lot of difference in the weeks I practise compared to the weeks I don't. My gestures and speaking voice are more natural. My mind has begun to believe that this new skill is something I can do. And I'm one heck of a lot less nervous.

So never forget. Your mind is the key not only to overcoming nerves, but to developing proficiency in every aspect of public speaking. And the best part about it is that it's free!

HOW HAVE YOU BEEN CONDITIONED?

Now—it's check-up time. Take a look at the chart on the next page and see where your conditioning has placed you. Have your experiences affected your confidence?

YOUR ATTITUDE TO PUBLIC SPEAKING

Score 1 point for each of the factors that apply to you,
and then total each of your scores out of 10.

Negative factors

* Your parents were never involved in public speaking. ☐
* You were never involved in public speaking and debating at school. ☐
* You tried public speaking once or twice and were embarrassed. ☐
* Every time you spoke you read from a script and people were bored. ☐
* Nerves always got the better of you—or you were plain terrified! ☐
* Your family tended not to talk much about anything—deeds counted, not words. ☐
* Your friends regarded public speaking as 'sissy' or something the brainy kids did. ☐
* You were a shy child who hated being the focus of attention. ☐
* Your parents urged you to excel at sport rather than at academic or speaking skills. ☐
* You didn't feel confident about your use of grammar and vocabulary. ☐

TOTAL: _____ out of −10

Positive factors

* You come from a family which took public speaking for granted. ☐
* You took part in school debates and public speaking opportunities. ☐
* You tried public speaking and experienced success. ☐
* You mastered speaking from a few main points and established rapport with the audience. ☐
* You learned to deal with nerves and use the adrenalin for positive results. ☐
* You were always encouraged to vocalise your feelings. ☐
* Your friends admired those who could speak well. ☐
* You were a friendly child who enjoyed being the focus of attention. ☐
* Your parents encouraged you to have a go at everything. ☐
* You felt confident about the way you handled words. ☐

TOTAL: _____ out of +10

Well. Did you end up with a score of minus ten, thanks to your conditioning? Or was it a plus ten? Or somewhere in between?

This will give you a rough idea of why you feel the way you do about public speaking: confident, terrified or somewhere in between. The bottom line is:

Speaking is a skill, and skills can be learned.

Suppose you decided one day that you wanted to learn to skydive. Would you expect to turn up at a skydiving site, pay your money, strap on a parachute and go up? If so, you'd be doomed to disappointment. No one would let you jump out of a plane without learning a few skills first. You'll find you have to jump off a chair and practise falling 200 times first!

Public speaking involves the same mastery of skills, step by step. So first, be aware of how your life experiences have formed your attitude to public speaking, and decide to start mastering those skills from wherever you stand right now. Remember:

No one is a 'born' public speaker.

With practice, you can be as good as anyone.

IN SUMMARY...

★ Writing and delivering a speech is a straightforward process.
★ No one is a 'natural-born speaker'.
★ The magic words are:

I want to.

★ Relaxation is an important part of developing effective communication skills.
★ Before speaking, picture yourself being relaxed, confident and entertaining.

- ★ To control nerves: breathe deeply and count slowly to 4. Then tell yourself:

    I am in control.

- ★ Don't try to be word perfect.
- ★ If you are an inexperienced public speaker, don't try too much too soon. Build up slowly to longer speeches and bigger audiences.
- ★ Be natural.

4

DIFFERENT STROKES FOR DIFFERENT FOLKS

Once when travelling through Houston, Texas, I noticed a massive neon sign. It read:

WE NEVER PLAN TO FAIL—WE FAIL TO PLAN

This is so true. Never more so than when you apply it to public speaking. So before you speak anywhere you should help yourself to plan your speech properly by asking yourself three important questions:

1. What is the purpose of my speech?
2. Who is my audience?
3. Is this speech right for me?

KNOWING YOUR PURPOSE

In answering this question you might find the table below helpful. It divides speeches into three classes according to the *purpose* of the speech: a 'thanks' type speech, an 'information' type speech and a 'motivational' type speech.

WHAT IS THE PURPOSE OF MY SPEECH?

Is my purpose:

	Yes	No
1. To thank?		
★ To propose a toast?	☐	☐
★ To introduce somebody?	☐	☐
★ To propose a vote of thanks?	☐	☐
2. To inform?		
★ To deliver a lecture?	☐	☐
★ To instruct a group?	☐	☐
★ To give an 'armchair' talk?	☐	☐
3. To motivate?		
★ To sell an idea?	☐	☐
★ To produce action?	☐	☐
★ To promote better performance?	☐	☐

A look at the 'thanks' type speech

This type of address should be short, crisp and to the point. Here's a useful table to consult:

WHAT SHOULD I INCLUDE?

A 'thanks' type speech might include:

1. Toasts:

    ★ light family detail
    ★ humour
    ★ common-sense

2. Introductions:

    ★ the good qualities or achievements of the speaker

3. Votes of thanks:

    ★ positive points of the address
    ★ a repeat of some of the speaker's words
    ★ a conclusion

Toasts

Use family humour, but *don't* indulge in long, boring reminiscences. In general, keep toasts short. They should rarely exceed three minutes. *And don't forget to propose the toast at the end of your speech.*

Introductions

Your job in this case is to introduce a person to their audience.

* **DO:**
  — get sufficient background knowledge of the person to give the audience a true idea of *who* they are and *what* they have done
  — highlight the person's authority on the subject of the speech.

* **DON'T:**
  — pre-empt the speaker's own address.

* **CONCLUDE:**
  — by saying: 'I would like you to join me in a warm welcome to our guest speaker...'

When you are faced with the task of introducing someone, it helps to remember the acronym BIN. This represents the speaker's:

Background

Interests

Name

BIN. Such a simple word—yet it makes your task so much simpler! Even if you are asked to introduce someone at the last minute at the RSL club, you can quickly scrawl 'BIN' on a coaster and away you go. What is the background of the person you have to introduce? What are their interests, and how will what they have to say be of interest to this specific audience? Finally, check that you have the speaker's correct name. That will give you plenty of ammunition for any introduction.

Here are some examples of good and bad introductions.

A bad introduction

Our special guest today is Stephen Dawson. Stephen Dawson has a PhD in earth moving. Mr Dawson completed his major in this subject at the University of Queensland where he spent another seven years researching the impact on the environment. Mr Dawson has written several books and is considered a world authority on this interesting subject.

Mr Dawson addressed an international conference last year on this same subject. Please welcome Mr Dawson.

A good introduction

Our special guest today completed her studies at the age of 22 and for the past 10 years has authored numerous books and spoken at international conferences. Her research is acclaimed by all as being right on the cutting edge.

She manages a team of 30 research assistants who are involved in the day-to-day work of managing the environment. This year alone she will address 10 000 people on how we can all do it better.

Please welcome our very special guest Dr Janice Dawson.

Votes of thanks

Remember that it's not your job to be the local critic. Refer to the good points of the speaker. (Make them up if they don't have any.) Be sure that you do your job—which is to *thank* the speaker for the time they have given and for their address.

Conclude by saying:

I ask the members of this group [or association] to join me in extending this vote of thanks to Ms Jane Bloggs by acclamation.

Here are some examples of good and bad votes of thanks.

A bad vote of thanks

Madam Chair, Ladies and Gentlemen: This is not my usual sort of thing, so I will be brief and to the point. I enjoyed our speech on the environment…however, there are a few points that I disagree with our speaker on, but I would like to thank him anyway. Would you please thank Mr Dawson in the usual way.

A good vote of thanks

Madam Chair, Ladies and Gentlemen: The record crowd in this room this evening is a reflection of the calibre of our dynamic guest speaker. Dr Dawson has given us 45 minutes of thought-provoking, stimulating information on how you and I can do anything better. You could have heard a pin drop in this room when she said, and I quote, 'Each of us is responsible for our own behaviour; we can make the change.' Throughout this address she made us think. We now know what it is we have to do.

We thank you, Dr Dawson, for your time, your energy and your information. Please join me in carrying this vote of thanks by acclamation.

Never ask the audience to 'thank this speaker in the usual way'. For all you know, their usual way might be to throw something! Simply say 'I would like you all to thank this speaker by acclamation' and start off the clapping yourself. If the speaker was good enough, you should stand and ask the audience to stand too. Don't be afraid to ask for a standing ovation if the speaker has done an outstanding job.

A look at the 'information' type speech

There are three main types of speeches designed to impart information. They are *lectures*, *instructional* speeches and *'armchair'* talks. We'll take a look at each in turn.

Lectures

Lectures are a special type of communication. We assume that the person giving the lecture is an authority on their subject. That might very well be the case, but those listening end up not caring about all that expertise. They're too busy fighting to stay awake. In a lecture, the speaker must make a special effort to engage the audience.

What sort of speech should a lecturer give if they really want to get information across in a way that will interest their audience?

★ They use *examples*.
★ They try to engage the interest of their audience.
★ They look for indications that they are being *understood*.
★ They respond to signs of confusion or boredom by swiftly adapting the presentation as they go along.

The instructional speech

If the aim of your speech is to *teach* your listeners something, then you will want to make sure that they *remember* what they hear.

To help them remember:

* Break the detail into sections.
* Number each section or use colour codes to show how each section is related to the topic as a whole.
* Support your talk with visual or printed aids—don't just *tell* them, *show* them! Use a white board, visual displays or overhead transparencies.
* Retention is based on repetition. If you want your listeners to remember what you've said, tell them what you are going to say, say it, then tell them you've said it! *Repeat, repeat, repeat.*

The 'armchair' talk

Don't be misled by the title of this type of talk. It *doesn't* mean that you are going to plonk yourself down in an armchair and chat away from a seated position. This type of talk is a matter of style and personality—as relaxed as though you were talking to friends from an armchair.

The 'armchair' approach should only be used if you are sure that the content of your talk will carry you through. It was about 10 years ago that I first saw how, in certain circumstances, this could be a very powerful approach. But be warned: you need the right material.

John Lough was a man who had that material. Let me tell you his story.

John and Margaret Lough had a child with leukaemia. After a lot of heartache and stress, they were able to accept that sad fact, but they wanted to do something about it. They approached Wollongong Apex Club to promote the issue as a fund-raiser. Their story was powerfully persuasive: everybody became so emotionally involved in the issue that they 'sold' it not only to district but national levels of Apex. Finally, John was asked to speak to a record crowd of 300 people who would vote on whether this should become a national fund-raising scheme.

I coached John and helped him rehearse. I told him all the things he should do to put across a powerful presentation. 'Whatever you do,' I said, 'don't walk out there and be casual about things. Here's my book on public speaking...do this...don't do that...blah blah blah.'

'Yes, yes,' he said—and went out there and did it his way. On the night, as I sat there and watched, John ignored all the advice I'd given him. Instead, he walked up to the microphone and sat down. In a chair, just like Dave Allen.

Completely relaxed, John went on to tell his story simply, movingly, as though to a roomful of friends. To him, it was far too intimidating to try it any other way. What got the message across so powerfully was the passion of his message. In my 20 years of public speaking I've never seen anyone else do it.

For John, it worked. He got a standing ovation. You might be able to get away with that very casual approach in front of an audience too, but only when you have a definite empathy with them. Only when they can see and feel the passion, and experience the pain with you.

If you feel it fits, if you feel comfortable with it, there's certainly a place for it. Just remember, the effect of this approach is completely different from the formal speech. It doesn't suit every situation, though, so if this is your natural style you may have to adapt it to the situation. You could rearrange the furniture; taking the chairs out of rows and placing them in an informal grouping.

Try to create a loungeroom atmosphere—move closer to your audience; make sure there's no lectern between you and them.

A word of warning: Resist the temptation to ramble on and on. Even if you are an armchair speaker, you must know exactly what you intend to say.

A look at the 'motivational' type speech

Remember to apply the golden rule of speaking and ask: 'What is the purpose of this speech?' In this case your *broad* purpose will be to persuade people to act in a particular way.

Selling an idea

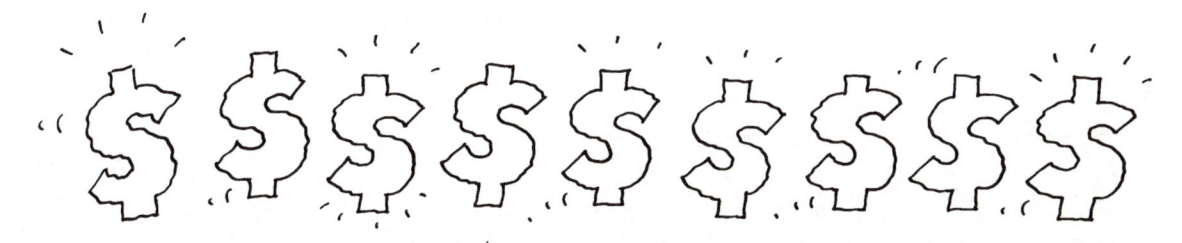

Okay, you want to sell an idea—but does your audience want to buy it? With this type of speech it is essential to look at things from your audience's point of view. You won't motivate people if they see you as a con artist. You must be credible. You must be sincere. You must be genuinely committed to the ideas you are expressing.

Producing action

As an experienced adjudicator, I can assure you that it is the *sincere* speaker who is always the most persuasive, convincing and effective at swaying the audience to their point of view.

It's difficult to sound sincere about something you don't understand. So research your topic thoroughly and prepare your speech carefully.

Promoting better performance

Why would your audience want to perform better? So they can be healthier? Wealthier? Happier? Whatever it is, show how increased performance will help them achieve it.

Every one of us will accept someone else's ideas *if they lead us to fulfil our own wants and desires*. Look for this angle in whatever content you present in your speech.

KNOWING YOUR AUDIENCE

The type of speech you choose, like the clothes you choose to wear, will depend on the occasion. Although most speeches have a standard structure, *the exact way to build your speech, and the exact words you use, will depend on the audience*.

Before you even *think* about writing a speech, ask questions about the audience's wants, needs, problems and achievements.

By doing that, you'll know how to best structure your speech to reach their hearts and minds. Your speech will virtually write itself.

Let's imagine you have just been invited to talk to the local rugby club about fund-raising. The first thing you should do is this: ask for the names of three people from that club to phone. In that speech, you're going to be selling yourself to them—your expertise, your ideas, your personality. So, like any salesperson, you should be doing a needs analysis to prepare for the sale! Do your pre-call planning.

Different Strokes for Different Folks

Here is a convenient form to use:

WHO ARE THE PEOPLE IN YOUR AUDIENCE?

1. What age group are they?
   _____

2. What do they want to hear from you?
   _____

3. What are their most pressing needs?
   _____

4. What problems need solving?
   _____

5. Who or what do they admire?
   _____

6. What do they consider important?
   _____

7. What information do you have about any of the individuals in the group?
   _____

When you have this information, you are in a good position to start planning your speech. When you begin to speak, you will immediately be able to show that you know and understand who they are and what they want. That will do a great deal to endear you to them.

Years ago, I was invited to listen to a speaker talk about the role of service clubs. He was going to be speaking to a very motivated group who had just finished raising a lot of money.

I sat there open-mouthed as I heard him say: 'The trouble with service clubs is that they are contented to sit on their backsides and not do anything!'

Obviously his ploy was to use shock tactics to make everyone sit up and take notice. Unfortunately, it backfired. As he went on, it was plain to everyone in the room that he had no idea what they had just achieved. As a result, there was an invisible wall between the speaker and his audience, and it stayed there.

What he *should* have said—and undoubtedly would have, had he done his homework—was something like: 'I congratulate you on your remarkable achievement in raising *x* amount of dollars. It is an effort that many other service clubs would do well to emulate...'

Today, you have to know more about your audience than you ever did. Regardless of where you go and to whom you speak, you should be doing your homework. Make it a rule:

HOMEWORK BEFORE MOUTHWORK.

IS THIS SPEECH RIGHT FOR YOU?

Doing your homework applies to more than just determining your purpose and finding out about the people in your audience, however. There are three other things you should consider before turning up to speak:

★ Are you the right person to give this speech?
★ Is it convenient for you to give it?
★ What is the venue?

Different Strokes for Different Folks

Use the following checklist to make sure a speech is right for you.

IS THIS SPEECH RIGHT FOR YOU?

1. When is it?

    Day: _____
    Time: _____
    Date: _____
    Time given to me: _____

2. Where is it? _____

3. What is it? _____

4. Why is it being held? _____

5. Who will be there? _____

6. Other information:

    —Location of venue: _____
    —Nature of venue: _____
    —Seating: _____
    —Acoustics: _____
    —Resources available: _____
    —Type of function: _____
    —My role: _____
    —Purpose of function: _____
    —How many people? _____
    —Background of audience: _____
    —VIPs expected: _____

Continued…

IS THIS SPEECH RIGHT FOR YOU?

7. Things to consider:

	Yes	No
—Is it convenient, given other commitments?	☐	☐
—Is preparation time adequate?	☐	☐
—Is it easy to get there?	☐	☐
—Is it suitable?	☐	☐
—Is it flexible?	☐	☐
—Can I get what I need?	☐	☐
—Are microphone facilities available if required?	☐	☐
—Can I contribute?	☐	☐
—Am I the best person?	☐	☐
—Is it clear to the organisers?	☐	☐
—To me?	☐	☐
—To the audience?	☐	☐
—Is my expertise in the area greater than theirs?	☐	☐
—Am I confident I have something worthwhile to say?	☐	☐

Thorough preparation is the hallmark of the capable speaker. Such preparation takes time—to research the topic, to gather facts, and to think about ways of presenting those facts.

All this spadework might seem a bit tedious, but the payoff is worth it. When you know your purpose, your audience and whether a speech is right for you, the foundations are in place for a well-designed speech.

IN SUMMARY...

In this chapter on planning your speech, we have covered most types of speeches you are likely to want to give or be asked to give, and the importance of knowing your audience and whether a speech is right for you. In the next chapter, we'll have a look at how to *structure* your speech. Before speaking *anywhere*, ask yourself:

1. What is the purpose of my speech?
2. Who is my audience?
3. Is this the right speech for me?

In determining the purpose of your speech, remember:

★ There are three main types of speeches:

— the 'thanks' type speech
— the 'information' type speech
— the 'motivational' type speech.

★ Toasts, introductions and votes of thanks are the three main 'thanks' type speeches.
　If you are proposing a toast, don't exceed three minutes.
　To introduce a speaker, use the BIN formula—Background, Interests, Name.
　When proposing a vote of thanks, don't criticise the speech—refer to the good points of the speaker.

★ There are three main types of speech designed to impart information: lectures, instructional speeches and 'armchair' talks.
　Lectures use examples, statistics, facts.
　Instructional speeches are designed to teach—make sure listeners remember what they hear. Show, don't tell; repeat vital information.
　The 'armchair' talk means a relaxed, informal style, not speaking from a seated position. This doesn't suit every occasion.

★ The 'motivational' type speech should sell an idea, produce action or promote a better performance.

Before you *think* about writing a speech:

★ Find out about your audience—their wants, needs, problems and achievements.

★ Before you agree to speak, ask:
   — Am I the right person to give this speech?
   — Is it convenient for me?
   — What is the venue?

Remember that thorough preparation is the hallmark of the capable speaker.

5

STRUCTURING YOUR SPEECH

Now that you have done your homework—determined the purpose of your speech, who your audience is and whether the speech is right for you—you are ready to move on to the speech-building process. You need to be very clear on one thing from the start: even if you were to study public speaking for the rest of your life, the building blocks of preparing a speech would always remain the same.

No matter how many new tricks or fancy techniques you learn to entertain your audience, you'll come back to the same old elements: the *introduction*, the *body* and the *conclusion*.

JOTTING DOWN IDEAS

The good news is, you don't have to worry about what goes where in the initial phases of preparation. Right at the beginning, all you need worry about is getting down as many ideas as possible. You can expand on your ideas and decide where to put them later.

Start by asking yourself: What do I want to say to people? What's the most important point I want to make? What's the next most important point? What would I like them to know that will help them or educate them? What stories can I tell to illustrate my points and help them to understand? And—most important of all—what do my audience want to hear? If you have done all your homework about your prospective audience, the answer to that question will be easy.

Once you have a clear idea about:

★ what the audience wants

★ what you would like to share with them

it's time to start pushing those ideas around until some sort of structure evolves.

Just how you approach these early stages of speech-building depends a lot on the way you prefer to think things through. If you feel more comfortable listing ideas in a formal 1-2-3 pattern, go ahead. If you prefer to scribble down ideas haphazardly with asterisks and arrows and circles all over the page, do it that way.

It doesn't matter how the ideas are arranged, as long as you get them down. Don't bother with full sentences at this stage—you are after key points, main ideas, essential facts and so on.

When you have a list of ideas in front of you, look at it to see if there are any related points. Link them with arrows, or colour code them.

THE THREE 'W'S

Once you have some initial ideas jotted down, take three blank pages and head them:

Warm-up

What's in it for them

Wrap-up

The 'warm-up' will be your opening section—the one that will hook the interest of the audience.

The 'what's in it for them' section contains the main body of information.

The 'wrap-up' ties up everything neatly and gives the audience something to think about when you leave them.

On each sheet of paper, start sorting your ideas into the appropriate section. Remember it's early days yet: things can be changed around later.

To help you, here is a guide to what should go in each section—first, a handy speech planner that tells you the general content, then a more detailed treatment of the type of content you should be using.

YOUR HANDY SPEECH PLANNER

1. Warm-up (the introduction):

   ★ What's my hook? How do I develop it?

2. What's in it for them (the body)?

   ★ How does it relate to their needs/wants/interests?
   ★ What is the main information?
   ★ What related stories/analogies/examples will I use?

3. Wrap-up (the conclusion):

   ★ What *can* they do OR why do they need to act now OR what are the benefits for them in using these ideas?

The warm-up

Always acknowledge the person who has called you to your feet and thank them. Addressing people as 'Mister Chairman' or 'Madame Chair' is considered by many people to be outmoded. Today's approach is friendlier: it's okay to call people by their first names.

The warm-up is the 'getting to know you' section. It's here that you will establish a relationship with your audience. This is a critical part of your speech. It's here that your listeners will decide, within the first two minutes, whether they will tune in to your message or ignore it. You need to get their attention immediately.

The most basic consideration (and, surprisingly, the one that's often neglected) is to stand in a place where you can be seen and heard clearly. (Note: This place is not necessarily behind the lectern!)

Your opening words must be positive: you're delighted to be here; you're flattered to have been asked; you couldn't wait to meet them.

Never, never, never deliver an apology. Some speakers, either out of false modesty or nerves, seem to think it's necessary to beg forgiveness for being the replacement speaker, or for not being as entertaining as the previous speaker ('...although I can't hope to be as entertaining as Ms X was in the previous session, I'll try in my humble way...')

If you have conscientiously prepared a speech designed to offer something to the audience sitting before you, you have nothing to apologise for. Why plant negative expectations in the mind of the audience?

In your warm-up, make sure you acknowledge the group in such a way that they feel that you really know and understand them. Show that you've done your homework—that you are here especially to talk to them. Use phrases like:

I'm here to share with you...

My mission today is to present a few ideas for us to explore together...

I'm looking forward to discussing with you...

I'm delighted to be standing here in front of you...

I couldn't have been more pleased when (X) invited me to speak to you...

What a pleasure it is to be standing in front of such an enthusiastic crowd...

All of the above phrases show that you are thinking of the audience, not just of yourself. Show them how they can use the information you're putting across.

All those listeners out there, with their expectant faces turned to look up at you, are hungry for words they can identify with. They think:

What's in this for me?

Will I learn anything new? Hope she's interesting…

Here are a few helpful hints:

DO:

- Be friendly and low-key in your approach.
- Be easy, confident and positive. Expect your audience's attention and you are more likely to get it.
- Take your time. Make sure that they can hear you and understand you. Use lots of eye contact and pauses to maintain their interest. Make them feel comfortable and relaxed. Give them a chance to get to know you.
- Open your mouth to be heard!

DON'T:

- Antagonise them by coming on too strongly.
- Be negative and show your nervousness. If you don't seem to believe in yourself, your audience certainly won't believe in you.
- Rush through your introduction. If your audience has to struggle to follow your line of thought you will make them feel tense and confused.

Note:
> The actual preparation of the warm-up to your speech should be last. Certainly keep your introduction in mind, and know more or less where you intend to go with it—but don't develop any fixed ideas until *after* you have prepared the body of your speech. Even then don't be surprised if some last-minute changes are necessary to make sure that the tone of your introduction matches the identity of the group you are going to address.

The 'ABC' formula

Here is a quick formula to get your warm-up underway: the ABC formula. This is a formula I have used for many, many years. And I'm going to keep using it—because it works!

'A' is for attention

- ★ Acknowledge the speaker who called you to your feet.
- ★ Gain the audience's attention by always speaking from a position where you can be seen and heard.
- ★ Learn the five simple steps to getting started:
    1. As soon as your name is called to speak, sit still and count to 5. Get your breathing right. Be conscious of your breathing: hear the air going out.
    2. Relax. Actually say the word 'relax' as you're walking to the speaker's position.
    3. Look the audience in the eye and smile before you open your mouth.
    4. Open with a very clear voice.
    5. Start slowly. You'll feel more in control, and you will hold the attention of the audience more easily.

'B' is for break the ice

★ Use pleasant, warm words that allow your personality to shine through. For example:

> I'm absolutely delighted to be here—even though I may be shaking in my shoes.

'C' is for communicate

★ Many people start a speech by saying:

> I want to talk to you about...

Avoid that approach. Instead, try to communicate with a real idea of idea sharing. For example:

> My purpose here tonight is to share my ideas with you.

What's in it for them?

When you are ready to start writing the body of your speech, think 'Radio WIIFM'. One of Australia's marketing gurus, Winston Marsh, always tells his clients that:

> There's a new radio station called WIIFM—'What's In It For Me'!

What he's saying is that people are tuned for whatever seems relevant to their own lives. That's why the body of your speech should contain lots of 'WIIFMs': the more your listeners feel 'connected' to what you're saying, the more impact your message will have. And that's straight out of the mouths of the marketing people!

So start thinking of this part of the speech as 'what's in it for them'. Why will they want to listen to what you have to say? How will it relate to what is important in their lives?

This part of your speech is most important, and should be prepared first.

Most newcomers to speaking try to pack too many ideas into their speech. Look for just the best, most important, and most interesting ideas. Wherever possible, look for ways to relate the content to the audience.

The objective of the speech (and the magic question missed by at least half of the people who think they are good speakers) is:

How can I present this subject in a way that will interest the listeners?

For the sake of argument, let's suppose you are an expert at fishing. You might (God forbid!) tell your audience one of your Big Fish stories, but it's unlikely that it will interest *them*, no matter how memorable it was for *you*.

Do your listeners want to hear about The One That Got Away? It's unlikely.

Would they like to hear about where the big fish are and how *they* can catch them? *Much* more likely.

These tips will help you keep your presentation alive:

* *Keep it local.* Make sure your facts are local and uncomplicated.
* *Keep it simple.* No sweeping statements. No overload of information. Don't give your listeners *too* much to think about.
* *Identify.* Use words that identify the audience with your subject. That way you have them hanging on your next sentence. Make them feel that they are part of your subject.

A useful technique for building and structuring the body of your speech is the ERS technique.

The ERS technique

You have already jotted down every point you can think of. Now choose the most important. Then the next most important. And so on,

Structuring Your Speech

until you have five. (Any more than five and you risk overwhelming the audience with too much information.) Think: *what must my audience know?*

Now build five mini-speeches around your five key points. How do you structure your mini-speeches? Try the ERS model:

E   Explain it

R   Reinforce it

S   Sell it

Explain it
Make a few statements related to the main point of the mini-speech. (Or ask and then give answers to some provocative questions.)

Reinforce it
Offer a short anecdote to illustrate your point. Tell the story, don't read it. Or alternatively perform a short demonstration. Or offer facts and statistics to back up your point, but make sure they are interesting and relevant to the audience.

Sell it
Make sure you've got the main point across to the audience by 'selling' it to them. Show them how the information will affect *them*.

This is a simple but effective technique. Follow the same ERS structure for each mini-speech and *voila!*—you have a watertight, carefully planned speech. Best of all, you need only have a small card in front of you with your five main points (or key words) on it. Since you are an expert on your topic, that's all you need to jog your memory. To make short work of structuring your speech, use this guide:

How to be the Best Speaker in Town

USING THE ERS SPEECH-BUILDING TECHNIQUE

My subject is:

My five main points are:

1.

2.

3.

4.

5.

My five mini-speeches are:

1.
    E
    R
    S

2.
    E
    R
    S

3.
    E
    R
    S

4.
    E
    R
    S

5.
    E
    R
    S

The wrap-up

The wrap up is where you should reinforce your ideas, to leave listeners with a lasting impression. It must be put clearly and simply. The last statement you make is likely to be the best remembered.

DO: Structure your conclusion along these lines:

Tonight I have tried to make you aware of the problem [whatever that might be]. I have shown you a solution [if there is one]. The decision to move one way or the other rests with you, the people involved. I must make my own decision [pause]… and you must make yours. [STOP!]

Another good idea is to adopt an old journalist's trick: link ideas at the end to ideas at the beginning for a nice 'circular' format. It ties things up neatly.

DON'T: Use old cliches like:

In summing up…

And in conclusion…

I would just like to add…

And don't ever end with:

Thanking you…

Signposts

'Signposting' means signalling to the audience that you are about to wrap-up. Do this by restricting your movements, and make it quite clear from your voice that you are in the 'summing-up' phase.

By standing still you draw their eyes back to you. Then make sure you use very powerful emotive words like:

Even if you leave this room today and forget most of the things I've suggested to you…[pause…slow down everything: pace, movements, voice etc.]…please remember this [pause…make significant eye contact]…[make your statement and finish].

Don't say 'thank you'. Just maintain eye contact for a moment longer, then leave. The impact will be much greater than if you add something that sounds weak after your final statement.

A WORD ABOUT HUMOUR

One of the most common mistakes made by speakers (and not just new speakers) is attempting to win over an audience by telling a series of jokes. Speakers do it to try to make an audience feel comfortable with them.

Usually, it has just the opposite effect.

Even professional comedians confess to having difficulty with timing on occasions. They'll tell a joke and it will fall flat—sometimes because of timing, sometimes because it's the wrong type of joke for that audience, sometimes because listeners have heard it once too often.

If you tell a joke and it falls flat, everyone's embarrassed—and you're off to a weak start which could wreck the whole speech.

By all means, use *humour* if you think it will enhance your speech. It's a great aid in motivating people. But don't think that five successive one minute jokes will do the job for you. Remember, humour should support your theme, not dominate it. The reason for your humour must be clear. Follow the '7 Rules of Humour'.

THE 7 RULES OF HUMOUR

1. *Humour must fit you.* Resist the temptation to take something that works for someone else and adapt it to suit your presentation. If it's not something that comes naturally to you, avoid it like the plague. If humour of any kind doesn't come naturally to you, find some other way of entertaining the audience.
2. *Humour must fit the audience.* You won't get anywhere by using humour that is over the head of your audience, or too risque. Learn to judge the audience and decide on the type of humour they'd go for.
3. *Humour must fit the occasion.* Not all presentations are suited to the use of humour. You can keep the audience interested without making them laugh.
4. *Humour must be on you.* I can talk about my flat feet, I can talk about my balding head, and I can talk about my own excess weight—and people will smile with me. They won't be so ready to smile if I take the mickey out of someone else's thinning hair or spare tyre, though. Humour against yourself will usually earn a laugh and draw people to you.
5. *You must think it's funny.* Resist the temptation to use someone else's joke simply because it got a laugh for them *if you didn't think it was funny*. If you don't trust the humour, it will come across in your presentation. You will be left standing there feeling a real goose while the audience winces—or gives a sick chuckle in sympathy.
6. *Humour must come from your experience.* Rather than use a joke, keep notes about genuinely funny things that have happened to you, or events that you witnessed. People always like 'real stories'. You won't forget the punchline, either.
7. *Humour DOES require practice!* To be delivered effectively, humour requires practice. Even professional comics know that. They practise and practise, changing their timing here and a word or two there, until they get just the effect they want. Your use of humour will become better with practice—you develop more of a sense of timing, and an appreciation of what will make an audience laugh.

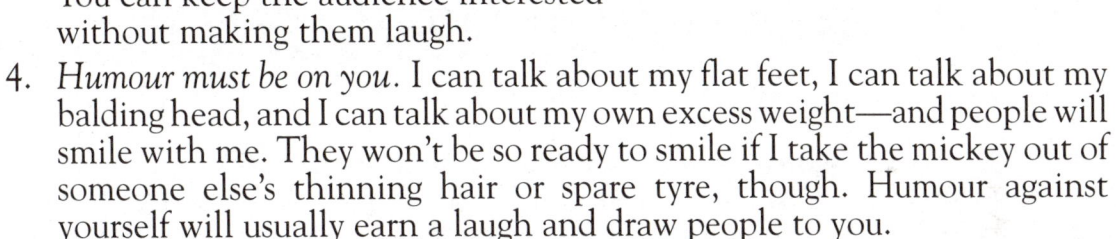

WRITING OUT YOUR SPEECH IN FULL

Even though you will later reduce your speech to a few key words and phrases using the ERS technique, it is always best to write it out in full first.

Why? Isn't that a waste of time?

No, it isn't. For the very good reason that writing out your speech in full forces you to organise your thoughts and write a smooth, logical presentation. You might find you want to edit your speech and move things around to be more effective. You might find a great opening line in the middle, or the perfect punch line five minutes from the end.

You will also have a great deal more confidence in yourself if you write out your speech in full. You will know what you want to say and how to say it. Speakers who think they can 'wing it' with a subject they know well often find themselves looking at a key word, then 'um' and 'er' while they try to think on their feet of how best to present a point.

Finally, here is a checklist for your speech:

A CHECKLIST FOR YOUR SPEECH

	Yes	No
★ Have you hooked the audience's interest with an effective warm-up?	☐	☐
★ Have you told the audience what's in it for them?	☐	☐
★ Have you reduced the body of your speech to five main points using the ERS technique?	☐	☐
★ Have you led slowly and logically into your presentation?	☐	☐
★ Does your speech have *balance* between stories, facts, statistics, jokes, examples and information?	☐	☐
★ Have you used suitable anecdotes to illustrate a point?	☐	☐
★ Have you reinforced your views with facts and reasoning?	☐	☐
★ Have you a definite message and have you presented it clearly?	☐	☐
★ Do you conclude by reminding the audience of your main message and/or key points?	☐	☐
★ Do you finish on a positive note?	☐	☐

IN SUMMARY...

- ★ Divide your speech into three parts: the *warm-up*, the *what's in it for them* and the *wrap-up*.
- ★ **DO:** be friendly, confident and positive; take your time; open your mouth to be heard.
- ★ **DON'T:** come on too strongly; be negative; rush through your introduction.
- ★ To keep your presentation alive: keep it local; keep it simple; help the audience to identify with your subject.
- ★ Choose five main points—any more and you risk overwhelming the audience. Think: *what must my audience know?*
- ★ Build five mini-speeches around the main points using the ERS technique: Explain it; Reinforce it; Sell it. Explain it by summarising the main point of the mini-speech. Reinforce it by using a short anecdote, an example, a demonstration, or by offering relevant facts and statistics. Sell it by showing how the information will affect your audience.
- ★ Don't use cliches like 'and in conclusion' to wrap up your speech.
- ★ Use humour if you think it is appropriate. But remember the '7 Rules of Humour': it must fit you, it must fit the audience, it must fit the occasion, it must be on you, you must think it's funny, it must come from your experience and it requires practice.

6

WRITING A SCRIPT

Not everyone will need or want a script. This chapter is for those who need a stepping stone between reading a speech and using minimal or no notes, and for those who consider the decision to be clear-cut: no script, no speech!

Apart from sheer terror at the idea of speaking without detailed notes, there are other reasons for needing a script. Sometimes conference organisers ask that you send them the text of your speech in advance, so they can publish it in a set of conference papers.

Sometimes *you* can make extra money by selling booklets containing your speech and other useful information.

It's also wise to write out your speech in full if you are trying to convey complex ideas to the audience. In this case, it's all too easy to tie yourself up in knots if you try to wing it.

Writing a Script

The following checklist will help you decide if you:

★ need a script
★ have prepared your speech properly for easy reading.

A 7-POINT CHECKLIST: PRODUCING AND READING FROM SCRIPTS

Ask yourself:

		Yes	No
1.	Do you need a script for:		
	— nerves?	☐	☐
	— conference papers?	☐	☐
	— imparting complex information?	☐	☐
2.	Do you need to write your speech first (for publication) and then adapt it for oral presentation?	☐	☐
3.	Have you used a large typeface for your script?	☐	☐
4.	Have you inserted slashes in places:		
	— where you need to take a breath?	☐	☐
	— where you want to make eye contact?	☐	☐
5.	Have you practised the 'skim-and-speak' technique?	☐	☐
6.	Have you repeated or restated important points?	☐	☐
7.	Have you a personal story or two ready to break up your script reading?	☐	☐

If you intend to take a script up to the podium with you, here are some tips on the best way to handle it.

DON'T READ YOUR SCRIPT WORD FOR WORD

There is no doubt that there are some very popular speakers who always use a script. However, the reason they are so popular is only in part due to the content of the script. The other reason for their success is this: they do not *read* from the script. Instead, they have mastered the art of skimming the script before them so that they appear to be talking to the audience. They make plenty of eye contact.

Less practised speakers are likely to find they have lost their audience in the first 60 seconds. That is because they are totally preoccupied with 'keeping their place' rather than whether the audience is awake and interested. The people in front of them feel that they might as well be given a copy of the speech to take home with them to read.

IS IT WELL-SPOKEN OR WELL-WRITTEN?

The most important thing to remember is that we speak in one way and write in another. What looks good on a page doesn't necessarily sound good when you try to speak it.

The rule for preparing a speech that is going to do double duty—that is be spoken and also published—is to write it for publication *first*. When you do this, strive for an easy style, use lots of white space to make it easier to read, and use plenty of examples and anecdotes. This will not only make it easier to read, it will make it easier for you to convert it into a script that you can read fluently from the podium. 'Prepare the script so it sounds natural', discussed below, will help you here.

A word of warning: *timing* is of vital importance. Leave yourself plenty of time to get through all the material in the published speech. Not everybody will buy a set of conference papers or the text of individual speeches. Your audience may feel cheated if they discover that those who buy the conference papers get extra information.

DON'T APOLOGISE

I'm not very good at public speaking, so I hope you'll bear with me while I read this to you…

These are words that should never be heard from the mouth of any speaker. Just as you do not apologise for any speech you are going to deliver, you do not *ever* apologise for using a script. If you do, your audience will start by wondering just how bad you are going to be.

Do you want them to be sitting there *expecting* you to bore them? Or to go away feeling cheated? Or even sorry for you? None of these reactions is desirable.

Rest assured, if you learn how to use a script properly it's on the cards *they'll* never notice.

USE A LARGE TYPEFACE

You should be able to comfortably read a script from a distance of at least 1 metre, and you will probably find that lower case type is much easier for the eye to decode than upper case. (See for yourself—try typing out a paragraph of a novel in capital letters then compare it with the original. Which is more comfortable to read?)

You could hand-print your script in large letters, but that is very time consuming. It is also difficult to print neatly enough for easy reading. By far the best option is to use a word processor with a good printer. Using this method, you can choose a large point size when you print out your script.

Here is an opening paragraph from a script that formed the basis of one of my audio tapes. Compare the typed version with the alternative, printed out in 18 point Times script:

SAMPLE SCRIPT 1

All right.

We've talked about prospecting for new business.

We've talked about the importance of building rapport with your clients.

We've talked about exploring their needs.

Discovering what they want.

But sooner or later / you will get to the point / where you must present your product or your service / to the customer.

And that's / what we'll talk about / on this tape.

Let me start / by telling you a story. Right now / I'm renovating a rat-infested hovel / that I bought in Sydney.

It's going well. My architect / has done an excellent job. The builders are great.

Now look at the 18 point Times version which follows. Which would you find easier to read from in front of an audience? There's quite a difference!

SAMPLE SCRIPT 2

All right.

We've talked about prospecting for new business.

We've talked about the importance of building rapport with your clients.

We've talked about exploring their needs.

Discovering what they want.

But sooner or later / you will get to the point / where you must present your product or your service / to the customer.

And that's / what we'll talk about / on this tape.

Let me start / by telling you a story. Right now / I'm renovating a rat-infested hovel / that I bought in Sydney.

It's going well. My architect / has done an excellent job.

The builders are great.

You will notice other differences from a normal speech, too. On the sample script above, you will notice that it has been rewritten to sound natural when it is read aloud—which brings me to the next point—building rapport.

BUILD RAPPORT WITH PERSONAL STORIES

There are two excellent reasons for breaking your delivery in a couple of places to relate personal stories. Firstly, you can maintain full eye contact for the duration of the story. There's no better way to seize the attention of the audience. Second, personal stories are so familiar to you that there's no need to write them out. Just one word or phrase in bold type (maybe highlighted) will be enough to remind you. Because you're telling the story instead of reading it, your delivery will instantly become warmer. It's just like telling a story to a group of friends.

Although you need only a word or two to jog your memory in the script in front of you, don't forget to write out the story in full if your speech is going to be published!

PREPARE THE SCRIPT SO IT SOUNDS NATURAL

To get the script you see above to the point where it is now, I reworked it several times. I first wrote it out as naturally as possible, in a chatty style that would be easy to read. I wanted to sound as though I was talking to someone.

Then I practised reading it out loud. I pretended the audience was right there in front of me, emphasised the points I wanted emphasised, and made notes about the changes to words and phrasing as I went.

Sometimes I chose to write phrases rather than sentences. Sometimes I repeated a phrase for emphasis, or to drive a point home. And at other times I changed a statement to a question to add interest and get the audience thinking.

I also tried to write visually—to choose words that would create a picture in people's minds. If you try to sell people vague, wordy concepts from the podium, you'll lose them while they engage in some mental juggling to try to understand. Here are some of the things you'll need to keep in mind:

* We speak in short sentences; we write in longer sentences.
* We speak for immediate comprehension, whereas when we write, people can re-read the material and refer to previous points.
* When we speak, we can use facial expressions, gestures and voice emphasis to enhance the message. When we write, words have to do all the work.
* Find a way of explaining difficult concepts without making the audience feel you're talking down to them. Use analogies, simple diagrams, and repeat the same information in a different way.

Finally, when I had the script reading as naturally as possible, I put in slash marks where I stopped to take a breath, or where I wanted to pause for effect. By doing that, even if I momentarily lost concentration I knew I could stop at a slash mark and the pause would sound natural. I could concentrate on delivery of the phrases and eye contact with the audience instead of the overall sense of what I was reading. And that is the final consideration when using a script—eye contact.

USE EYE CONTACT

This is probably the most important thing for you to keep in mind when you are working from a script. Eye contact forms a bond between you and the audience. If you break that bond, so that all they see is the top of your head as you concentrate on your notes, they'll stop looking at you.

Why should they pay attention to you when you're not even talking directly to them? They'll find it infinitely more interesting to read the program, or to look around them to see what other people are doing, or to talk to the person next to them. Or they'll drift off into a daydream—and you've lost them.

Lack of eye contact says:

I'm not interested in you.

It says:

I don't know if you're interested and I don't care.

It says:

This speech is not for an audience of real live people.

Obviously, if you're using a script, you are going to have to glance at it regularly. That's why you'll go to all the trouble of printing it in a large size print and putting slashes in to show where to pause. So learn how to use those pauses to your advantage.

Learn to skim read a phrase, then look at the audience and say it to them instead of reading it. If you're worried that you'll lose your place when you look up, rest your finger on the line you're reading.

When you have made eye contact, pause while you glance down to skim the next bit. Don't be tempted to pick up the pages and put them near your face to read from. *Skim, speak while making eye contact*, then *skim again*.

It takes practice to do this effectively, but it's worth the effort. And, finally, don't forget to mark out one or two places in the script where you can tell a familiar anecdote. By doing this you can maintain eye contact for several minutes before going back to the skim-and-speak technique.

A FINAL WARNING

Always check the final printout of your script before taking it up to the podium. Computers and printers are wonderful tools, but on occasions they can do dreadful things to your speech. It's too late to do anything about a missing page or garbled text if you're halfway through your speech.

IN SUMMARY...

- ★ There are several reasons you might want to write out your speech in full: for conference organisers to include in a set of conference papers, to impart complex information, or because you'd be totally unable to deliver a speech if you didn't.
- ★ Don't read your speech word by word (you run the risk of losing your audience).
- ★ If your speech is going to be published, write it for publication *first*, and script a revised version to read from *second*.
- ★ Never apologise for having to read your speech.
- ★ Use a large typeface in lower case for ease of use while you're using the skim-and-speak technique.
- ★ Write your script so that when you read it, it will sound as much like normal speech as possible. Use short phrases and sentences; separate with slash marks where you want to take a breath or make eye contact.
- ★ Break up your reading with personal stories.
- ★ Always maintain eye contact.
- ★ Master the skim-and-speak technique: skim each sentence (or two), then look up and *speak* it rather than read it.
- ★ Always check your script *well* before you take it up to the podium, to avoid being caught with missing pages or computer glitches that mean you've lost half the speech.

7

KNOWING WHAT TO SAY—KEEPING A SPEECH FILE

When you're still shaking at the knees about giving your first speech, it probably seems incredible that you will one day have a file drawer full of old speeches. Believe me, that day will come a lot sooner than you think. *Never throw out a speech*. You can use it as a basis for another, use parts of it that worked well, or, at worst, use it as a model of what *doesn't* work for you!

File your speeches under subject or purpose. In this computerised age, you might like to keep your speeches on disk. Word processors are wonderful for 'cutting and pasting' bits and pieces of two or more related speeches to come up with a completely new one. As you give more and more speeches, you will find that your work is halved. Sometimes better than halved; you may be able to use an 'old' speech as is.

Even if you prefer to keep your speeches on disk, you will probably find it easier to flip through and read printed copies of previously given speeches rather than scroll through computer files. Just how you file your old speeches is a matter of personal preference—you might like a row of folders labelled with subjects; you might prefer suspension files.

Your speech file will contain more than just old speeches. If you spend just a little time regularly filing information that attracts your interest on a range of subjects, you'll find your files worth their weight in gold when it's time to write a new speech.

Here are some tips for timely topics.

CLIP AS YOU READ

Most of us scan the morning and weekend papers and buy the odd magazine. What happens to those papers? They end up at the tip or in the recycling bin—along with that article you meant to clip and save.

It makes sense to keep a pair of scissors handy to clip out articles as you see them. Of course, this doesn't always work in practice—family members usually prefer to read newspapers without mysterious holes in them. But when you say: 'I'll clip it later,' you usually forget, right?

The solution:

* keep a highlighter pen handy instead of the scissors, and mark the article so you can find it quickly later, or
* keep a notepad and pen just for the purpose of noting article topics and page references each morning.

Then (and this is the hard part) discipline yourself to go through the newspaper pile every couple of days and clip those articles when everyone else has finished with them.

FILE AS YOU GO

Anyone who has ever started a collection of interesting material knows the next pitfall. You end up with a teetering pile of yellowing newsprint a kilometre high. The family gets sick of moving it from shelf to desk to floor to cardboard carton. Then comes speech-writing time and you look hopelessly at the huge pile of clippings and just *know* that you'll never be able to find that funny article on trekking through the wilderness anyway...

The solution: A two-step filing procedure. First, use a cardboard envelope (things fall out of folders) as a temporary measure. Toss in all articles as you clip. Second, use a more permanent and organised filing system: file under topics/occasions/themes/humour or whatever suits your organisational style. Go through your temporary file every couple of weeks (once a month at the outside) and sort your clippings into categories.

Every so often, go through your files and cross-reference your material. You'll be glad you did when you're in a hurry to find material and it's not where you expected to find it. Many items fit into several categories.

By the time you're ready to decide on a topic and write your next speech, your files will prove to be a rich resource.

COLOUR CODING: THE SPEAKER'S SECRET WEAPON

Colour is one of the most useful aids for efficient filing *and* for analysing the content of your speeches. Here are some suggestions that will make your life easier.

Use colour for ease in filing and finding

Try these hints:

* Use coloured folders or suspension files to indicate different topics—for example, green folders for stories and facts related to marketing strategies; red for customer service; blue for inspirational material; yellow for humour and so on.

* Use coloured dots or highlighter pens to make speeches and stories that could serve a dual purpose—for example, an anecdote about searching for and buying a new stereo could fit into speeches on marketing, customer service or negotiating skills.

Use colour to check that your speech is balanced

Here's a great way to ensure that you keep the attention of your audience from start to finish: colour code the different elements of your speech. Here's how you do it:

* Print out your speech in full.
* Mark the sections where you deliver *facts* in, say, green.
* Mark *stories* and *anecdotes* in yellow.
* Mark *humorous material* in red.
* Mark *examples* or *analogies* in blue.
* Mark *pauses* in orange.

There may be other elements your care to mark in different colours, but that will do to start with.

Now check through your speech again. What you *should* see are constant colour changes. If you see a chunk of yellow (a story) followed by pages of green (facts) with very few spots of orange (pauses) and a tiny dash of blue (examples or analogies), then it should be obvious your speech is bogged down in facts. You need something more to lighten it up and keep the audience entertained.

If necessary, rebuild your speech to ensure an even balance of components. Your aim should be to keep the audience interested at all times. And *that* means variety.

USE OTHER SPEECHES AS MODELS

Heard a good speech lately? When you get home, jot down the main idea, the main points, ideas about timing, humorous or inspirational anecdotes and so on. (*Never* pirate someone else's speech—there just might be someone in the front row of your audience who heard it too. Why ruin your credibility?)

It's a good idea to keep a section in your speech file entitled: *How others said it*. As well as noting the *content* of other people's speeches, make notes about structure and successful use of humour. If there were any parts of the speech that had the audience listening with bated breath, make a note about it. See if you can figure out why this happened. In other words, study both *content* and *technique*.

KEEP YOUR OWN IDEAS FILE

Keep small notepads and pencils everywhere—in the glove box of the car, by the bed, on the coffee table. Otherwise inspiration will strike when you have no means of writing it down. You 'know' you'll remember it because it was such a brilliant idea...but take it from me, you won't.

Naturally you won't let your notepads accumulate dust or disappear between the cushions of the lounge, will you? No! You'll write one idea per page and then tear the pages out regularly and file them in the same way as you do your articles. Or keep a separate 'one-line ideas' file.

USE COMPUTER TECHNOLOGY

These days, computers can do practically everything but deliver the speech for you. (Even that might not be too far away, at the rate things are developing!) So why not take advantage of their capabilities?

You will find that you use certain 'chunks' of information in speech after speech—facts, instructions, examples, tips and so on. Make life easier for yourself by storing these 'chunks' as separate files. Just copy them on to your computer clipboard from one document and paste them into another.

Your computer files should be arranged as meticulously as your folders and suspension files. Keep related 'chunks' of information together on the same floppy disk, as well as in the appropriate directory on your hard disk.

The more you speak, the more likelihood there is of having exactly the right 'chunk' of information ready to pull into your speech. With an appropriate transitional sentence or two, and some minor editing, there's a large part of your new speech ready to go.

COLLECT HUMOROUS ANECDOTES

These are everywhere. Friends and workmates tell funny stories about family life or recount tales they heard in the pub. You'll sometimes see short snippets in newspaper columns. Clip these (or write them down) ready to insert in a speech. (Note: it may be necessary to change names and details to protect people's privacy.)

When it comes to speech-writing time, you'll find that your files plus your own ideas equal magic. You see, the real problem is not that we don't have anything to say; it is to find a way of sinking shafts into our reservoir of knowledge and experience that will bring potentially fascinating material to the surface. As you mark, clip and file, you'll find that your own interests govern what you choose to file.

All of this is stored away deep in your subconscious. It will not be long before you will be saying to yourself: 'I've got three or four ideas for this speech...now which one will I use?'

RELATE YOUR SPEECH TO WELL-KNOWN VIDEOS AND MOVIES

A lot of the people you'll be speaking to will be familiar with the latest big screen movies and video releases. Even if they haven't got around to seeing them, it's likely they'll have heard others discussing them, or read the reviews.

By mentioning a scene from one of those movies, or quoting an extract of dialogue, you'll effortlessly create mental images in the minds of your listeners. The movie and the actors have done all the work for you!

Here's an example of how you might use a movie to illustrate your point. This example illustrates the idea that for our lives to change, we have to change:

In the movie Groundhog Day, *a television weatherman found himself living in a kind of hell. Every day, when he woke up, he found himself reliving the day before. At six o'clock every morning, he woke to the same music on the same radio station.*

Every night, he hoped to wake up to a new day and a different train of events.

But it didn't happen.

Until he learned that for his daily life to change, he had to change.

Most of us, at one time or another, have felt similarly trapped by our own lives. And like the weatherman in the movie, we'll be trapped in that grinding sameness, day in and day out, until we decide to change.

Every movie you see has an underlying idea (or premise) that could well be used in your speeches. Whenever you see a movie that moves you in some way—or that you just plain enjoyed—take some time after you see it to make notes. A few minutes of scribbling will pay off in one of your speeches.

Work out the underlying idea. Jot down clever lines of dialogue. Work out what a character's fatal flaw or saving grace was, or what motivated them to behave the way they did.

Then store your notes in the appropriate section of your files. Perhaps it will simply be a file called 'Movie quotes'. If the quote seems particularly relevant to one of your speeches on file, make a note such as 'See movie quote #46' on that speech.

These are just a few ideas that will make your speech files increasingly useful to you. You'll probably come up with other good ideas of your own.

Knowing What to Say—Keeping a Speech File

Here is a quick checklist to help you determine how organised you are:

HOW ORGANISED ARE YOUR FILES? A QUICK CHECKLIST

Score 2 for *Yes*, 1 for *Have begun*, and 0 for *No*.

	Yes	Have begun	No
1. Have you organised your speeches into content, topics or categories?			
2. Have you a system in place for clipping and filing useful material?			
3. Have you cross-referenced your files?			
4. Have you analysed your speeches for balance of content?			
5. Do you keep examples of other people's speeches and handouts?			
6. Do you keep notes on how other people deliver their speeches?			
7. Do you keep an ideas file?			
8. Have you organised your computer files?			
9. Do you know where to put your hand on any information you want (in both your hard copy files and your computer files, if applicable)?			
10. Do you collect examples of humour that will work for you?			
11. Do you relate your speeches to well-known movies and videos?			

Continued…

SCORING KEY

16–22: Excellent. Your files are well organised and should be a great time-saver and source of inspiration.

11–15: You have the basis of a good system in place. With a little more time and effort, you'll have a filing system that will work wonders.

6–10: It's time to devote a few days to streamlining your system. All the hard work you do in writing and practising speeches is going to waste if you don't have an efficient system in place for storage and analysis.

0–5: Hmmm. There's a long way to go here. Either you're an extraordinarily gifted speaker who doesn't need the same kind of help the rest of us mortals do, or you don't mind doing the same spadework every time.

IN SUMMARY...

- ★ File your speeches under subject or purpose.
- ★ Clip as you read. On the cover of the magazine or newspaper, note the page numbers of articles you want to clip. This lessens the risk of forgetting about them and throwing them out.
- ★ File as you go. Use two steps: first, clip and throw into a catch-all file or box; second, file regularly under the correct categories or topics.
- ★ Colour code your files for ease of location.
- ★ Use colour to analyse the balance of content in your speeches.
- ★ Use speeches by others as examples or models.
- ★ Keep an ideas file.
- ★ Use the benefits of computer technology to keep 'chunks' of information filed under suitable titles, ready to copy and paste into new speeches.
- ★ Collect humorous anecdotes and true stories; change names if necessary.
- ★ Relate your speech to well-known movies or videos for immediate impact.

8

PRACTISING YOUR SPEECH

So, now you have your speech, and you need to practise it. Don't leave your success as a public speaker to chance. Practising your speech will enable you to iron out any wrinkles so that you sound professional on the day.

You may be confident about your ability to carry it off...as long as the audience behaves itself. But what if they are unco-operative? Take heart. There's one practice method that will help you carry on speaking confidently over whispers, dropped cutlery, or people leaving the room.

DEAD SPACE

During practice sessions, one of your problems will be lack of an audience. The only one who is likely to have a sympathetic ear for your public speaking practice is good old Fido, the family dog (after he has been fed).

But don't be worried about speaking to an empty space. Imagine that the room is full of people, and you really are delivering your speech to them.

The secret is to rehearse in front of dead space. Not in front of a supportive friend or family member who will listen intently and smile back at you. Not in front of a mirror, where you'll look like a galah. You need to be able to practise being able to ignore *noise*.

You will find that music in the background will help. Many of my students have found that practising speaking over an existing noise level has been a very successful way of overcoming the distractions that often occur during public speaking performances.

Years ago I was in a public speaking contest in which I came second to a speaker whose topic was 'Black and White'. He dealt with the conflicts between people caused by differences in skin colour.

I took 'Nervous Tension' as my theme. I thought it was a clever speech, but since I came in second, it obviously wasn't good enough. Then I had a second chance, because both the first and second place getters were to go on to the next level of competition in Wagga. As far as I was concerned the contest in Wagga was just between the two of us. The others wouldn't get a look in.

I had two months to prepare, so it was back to the drawing board, or should I say the practice room—music and all!

I called in a friend of mine who was then recognised as the city's top speaker. He helped me rehearse my speech. At the beginning of our first practice session, we spent 20 minutes on just five words:

Mr Chairman, Ladies and Gentlemen…

This became so boring for all of us that his little daughter finally said in disgust: 'What about the boys and girls?'

But practice makes perfect, and so we continued, and finally the day of the competition arrived…

The scene: Wagga. No tin shed this time but a comfortable civic hall with a platform, and an audience of about 150 people. My major opponent was the third speaker. I was number five.

When I was called to the platform I felt very confident and ready to perform. Once I stood up and got underway, I felt that I had the audience in my control. The speech was being well received. Then total disaster struck! A portable table collapsed and crashed to the floor. The noise startled everyone and took their attention completely away from what I was saying.

But, thanks to my rehearsal, I was unshaken. I simply waited for everyone to settle and then picked up from where I'd left off.

At the end of the contest the adjudicator came to me and commented on my remarkable self-control under extraordinary circumstances. 'The accident didn't affect your presentation at all,' he assured me.

The result of the competition?

First: 'Black and White'.

Second: 'Nervous Tension'.

The better speaker won on both occasions. But I can thank my practice with music for my self-control. As I said to the adjudicator, it wouldn't have mattered if the roof had fallen in, I was in control of the situation—it did not control me.

A practice session

This is how you do it.

Face the wall and focus on a blank spot. Start speaking. Do your best to sound animated and interested with nothing but a wall staring back at you. Then it's time to up the ante: speak to the blank wall *with music playing*. The music should be just one notch up from a comfortable listening level.

If you can keep your cool and concentrate on being an entertaining speaker through all that, a few coughs and shuffles will be a piece of cake.

Apart from talking to the wall over the strains of slightly-too-loud music, what other aspects of public speaking will benefit from practice?

BODY CONTROL

To begin with let's concentrate on the art of controlling body movements from the eyes down. First, adopt a comfortable stance with your weight evenly distributed over both feet. Your chest and shoulders must be erect.

One hand should hold your notes, in case you won't have (or don't want) a lectern. The other should be held at waist height, ready to emphasise parts of your speech with natural gestures.

I was a nervous speaker at first. I just couldn't stand still. So I bought a large sheet of cardboard and drew my standing position on it. Then I placed it on the loungeroom floor and practised standing still while I spoke. I know there are many excellent speakers who move around as they speak, but they have learnt to distinguish between nervous, distracting movements and actions that will enhance their presentation. To begin with, it is better if you learn some control.

SEEING OURSELVES AS OTHERS SEE US

It's important to listen to yourself speak—and modern technology makes it possible. If you record yourself on tape and replay it, you can act as your own adjudicator. These are the sorts of questions you should be asking:

* *How is your tone of voice?* Is it varied and interesting, or dull and monotonous?
* *What about your rate of delivery?* Could somebody else understand what you were saying?

A cassette recorder gives you the chance to evaluate your own performance and rectify your mistakes before the real event.

The best aid of all is the 'mirror with a memory'—the video recorder. If you can have yourself recorded on video tape as you deliver your speech, you will be able to sit back and examine your own performance in full, realistic detail.

And if you don't like the image you project—if you feel that the speech is boring—you can bet that others are likely to feel the same way. It's time to work out how to improve on what you have done.

Even if you *do* like what you see, ask yourself if there's anything you can do to make it better. Nobody's perfect!

PRACTISE AT THE VENUE

To really give yourself the winning edge, practise at the venue.

I was working recently with the managing director of an organisation who was literally sick with nerves. His task was to introduce some famous high-powered speakers at a big conference in Sydney. I asked to see his speech.

One glance was enough to show me that there was nothing wrong with his material—not surprising, since he'd spent days preparing it. There was one major stumbling block—he hadn't practised the darn thing!

We whisked him straight to the auditorium where he would be speaking, knowing full well that the unknown always seems much more frightening than the known. He ran through his speech a couple of times and left in a much happier frame of mind. My client had discovered what all accomplished speakers know: the more you can simulate an event, the less nerves you'll have.

Before the moon landing, astronauts trained in a huge building fitted out to look like the moon. When they finally landed on the real thing, they felt right at home. It's exactly the same with public speaking. If you can manage to get there early—a few hours or even the day before—to run through your speech in the actual venue, you'll feel much more relaxed when you step up on the podium in front of your audience.

Apart from the advantages of practising your speech at the venue, it's essential that you do so for another reason—to make sure your audio-visual support is reliable. Even practised speakers sometimes lose sight of this, as I was reminded at the Asia-Pacific Sales Conference in 1993.

I was in Singapore with a group of experienced Australian and international speakers. It was the day before the conference, and naturally everyone was precoccupied with their own presentations: going through their material and dealing with nerves.

I suddenly realised that everyone had lost sight of the big picture. Instead of sitting there in isolation mentally rehearsing, we would have been better off down there in the auditorium, where 700 people were going to be sitting and listening to us the next day.

I took everyone to the auditorium to liaise with the audio-visual team—and discovered they didn't even have a running sheet. The technicians didn't know who was speaking when. They didn't know anything about individual speaking styles. It hadn't occurred to anyone that a speaker might want to walk down off the platform and move among the audience—which would require different sound equipment and a spotlight to follow them.

I suggested that everyone run through the first three minutes of their speech so they could test the sound, modulation and equipment. They paced out where they were going to be walking, because the day was going to be videoed.

We discovered other things that could be improved. They had allowed for just one podium, right in the centre of the stage. That meant that the person doing the introduction had to walk to the centre of the stage with their notes, then walk away from the centre to bring the guest speaker on. Nobody had ever suggested to them that they have two podiums, one at the left and one at the right, so that the person introducing needed to walk only about 1 metre *and* could leave all their notes there for the day.

Neither the organisers nor the audio-visual team had thought of such simple things as two podiums and a running sheet for the technical people. The lesson for everyone is *never assume*. Don't take it for granted that the organisers will know more about the speaking process than you do.

The more you can find out about what you have to do and how other people are going to help you do it, the better your presentation will be. In some cases, you might well be avoiding disaster.

To make the most of your talk, you need two things: the mental rehearsal and the physical rehearsal. If you can manage both, you're ahead of the game. *See* the crowd! *Feel* the noise!

Even if you can't get a *full* physical rehearsal, try to stick your head around the door and get a feel for the room and the acoustics. Walk in there and *hear* yourself.

Structure your first two minutes carefully, concentrating on the pace of your delivery. Take a friend and ask them to sit at the back of the room to give you feedback on how much projection you have to use. Unfortunately, most convention rooms aren't designed with speakers in mind: they're planned for the comfort of the listeners.

How to be the Best Speaker in Town

The rule of thumb I've come up with is this: if I'm speaking to more than 40 people, I use sound. Otherwise, if I'm projecting to a crowd that size for a half day or more, my voice is going to be bad news by the time I've finished. I don't take chances with what others might have organised, either. I've invested in my own reliable, easily portable sound system. Like the boy scouts, I'm prepared!

It can be very daunting speaking in an auditorium that can hold 1500 people as opposed to a room that holds 20. If you've seen it, at least you can picture it more clearly in a mental rehearsal.

PRACTISE, PRACTISE EVERYWHERE...

All this practice doesn't *have* to be at home or at the venue. Go to a park to practise if you want—so what if people stare at you? You'll get used to it! Anyway, psychiatrists say there's nothing wrong with talking to yourself; you only have problems if you start to listen!

Practise while you're driving your car, while you're lying in bed at night, while you're commuting by train. The more mental rehearsal you give a speech, the stronger your nerves will be on the day.

TEST YOUR SPEECH ON OTHERS

Another way to practise is to run through parts of your speech instead of the whole lot. For example, if you are going to tell a couple of anecdotes, tell them to friends, acquaintances and workmates first. Learn the most effective place to pause, and which words evoke the most effective images for your audience. If they laugh, note where they laughed.

If you will be quoting facts and statistics, run them by others first to see if they understand. If you will be explaining a technique, explain it first to others to make sure you have chosen the clearest and most persuasive way to get your message across.

There's no doubt about it, practice can be time-consuming and boring. There's also no doubt that practice will increase your confidence, enhance your delivery and get you asked back another day. So when you're going through your presentation for the umpteenth time, remember the words of George Bernard Shaw:

When I was a young man, I observed that nine out of ten things I did were failures. I didn't want to be a failure, so I did ten times more work.

YOUR PRACTICE CHECKLIST

	Yes	No

Movement

1. Can you speak without moving from one spot? ☐ ☐
2. Can you use controlled, meaningful gestures? ☐ ☐

Your voice (use a tape recorder)

1. Is your voice varied and interesting? ☐ ☐
2. Do you speak too fast? ☐ ☐
3. Do you speak too slowly? ☐ ☐
4. Do you clearly pronounce the final consonants of the words you speak? ☐ ☐
5. Do you use pauses effectively? ☐ ☐

The venue

1. Have you practised at the venue? ☐ ☐
2. Have you seen the venue? ☐ ☐
3. Have you checked that all necessary audio-visual equipment is there? ☐ ☐
4. Have you checked that all audio-visual equipment is working? ☐ ☐
5. Do you have a back-up procedure and alternative speaking aids in case of audio-visual equipment failure? ☐ ☐
6. Do you know:
   — exactly *when* you are speaking? ☐ ☐
   — how *long* you will be speaking? ☐ ☐
   — whether you need to allow for question time? ☐ ☐

Continued...

	Yes	No
7. Does the physical layout of the room (seating, placement of lectern and audio-visual equipment etc.) suit you? If not, can it be changed?	☐	☐

Practice

	Yes	No
1. Have you devoted extra practice time to the most challenging parts of your speech?	☐	☐
2. Have you tested humorous stories, examples and statistics you intend to use on colleagues or friends to see if they work?	☐	☐
3. Have you practised over noise?	☐	☐
4. Have you practised:		
— mentally?	☐	☐
— physically?	☐	☐

IN SUMMARY...

★ Practise over noise so that, on the day, you will be in control—no matter what happens.

★ Adopt a comfortable stance with your weight evenly distributed over both feet.

★ Learn to use controlled movements.

★ Tape your practice sessions so you can hear yourself as others hear you.

★ Practise at the venue (or at least visit it to familiarise yourself with the layout) *before* your actual delivery.

★ Never assume that the organisers will provide equipment or set it up the way you expect.

★ To make the most of your talk, you need both a *mental* rehearsal and a *physical* rehearsal.

★ If you will be quoting facts and statistics, run them by others first to see if they understand.

9

VOICE POWER

Rebekah Van den Berg teaches speech and drama in Sydney, Australia. She trained at Trinity College in London, and has worked extensively with America's leading 'voice guru', Rowena Balos.

As an accredited trainer with Dougmal Training Systems, Rebekah shows people how to make the most of their voice for public speaking and professional presentations. She shares her expertise and knowledge of 'voice power' in this chapter.

It was a Saturday afternoon when Doug asked me to write a chapter in his new book, *How to be the Best Speaker in Town*. I sat there smiling, playing with the froth on my skim milk cappuccino, waiting for the inevitable word 'instant' to escape from his lips. He said: 'Rebekah, we live in an instant society—computers, microwaves, faxes, mobile phones—blah blah blah. People need to learn to use their voice today—not in six to 12 months...'

Our conversation progressed into a game of verbal, somewhat bloody, tennis with any mention from me of words such as process, duration, time, being clearly shot back over the net with 'now', 'today', 'yesterday'. It was 40-Love in Doug's favour (The Vocal Barracuda!).

If your voice is not an ambassador for who you are and what you do...read on.

YOU ARE HOW YOU SOUND

Remember the cliche, 'you are what you eat'? The same is true for your voice. Your voice is reflective of your personality. Within ten seconds of opening your mouth, your listener intuits a mini-personal history—for example, education, health, status, how you feel about yourself, mental alertness. Your voice is the outward expression of your inner self.

An example

Jack is in telephone sales and he makes an average living. He speaks for eight hours a day with no awareness of how he sounds. Jack gets by.

Sitting next to him in his open plan office is his best friend Joe. They both started with the company at the same time, but Joe's commission is twice that of Jack's.

How can this be? They went to the same school, wear the same clothes, they dated the same girls. The only difference: Joe did a 10-week course in Voice Training.

Voice training can give you control of the impression you wish to create. *A dull voice leaves a dull impression*.

Think of Australia's wealthiest radio personality. Now think about, or should I say, feel his voice. Relaxed, friendly, secure, sensuous, hypnotic tone. In short, a vocal symphony that sounds like and says 'Trust me'. But—he wasn't born with that voice.

WHAT IS A GOOD VOICE?

Factors such as parents, environment and conditioning shape the sound of your voice. Infants and young children breathe naturally and produce free, musical, well-focused projected voices. As we grow and develop, we fall into a voice pattern and stay with it, believing it is our only option.

A poor voice is reflective of ingrained bad habits. Often the person with a poor self-image speaks with a dead, lifeless tone.

A profile of the Aussie voice

The Aussie voice tends to have a few distinctive characteristics:

* *Stiff and immobile lips*—this gives the impression of a reluctance to communicate; there is a tendency to speak in the back of the throat.
* *Jaw set and tight*—this leads to a flat, tense monotonous tone. The tongue has to work really hard to define the vowels in that limited, constricted space. It also makes the voice difficult to understand.
* *Starting a sentence loudly and fading away to nothing at the end.*
* *Habitually ending every sentence on a whiny pitch or a question mark.* As well as being irritating to the listener, this sends the subliminal message: 'I'm unsure of my information and I doubt myself.'

In essence, the Aussie speaker proudly wishes to convey this verbal portrait:

* I'm tough.
* I'm virile.
* I'm depressively unemotional.
* I'm deliberately casual.
* I'm basically stupid.
* I don't care.

Now, if you find this vocal approach works for you, don't read any further.

Most Australians equate 'speaking well' with changing your accent, elocution lessons, sounding 'posh' and 'girlie stuff'—perhaps an imitation of the English. These are a few of the many misconceptions of what good speech is—an unfortunate legacy of much bad voice teaching in the past.

Good speech has nothing to do with someone else imposing special sounds on you, or with making your speech conform to a particular pattern. A good voice is a voice not limited by physical tensions or lack of clarity. It is free and open to all its possibilities of range and powers.

Speaking well has to do with discovering the vitality of your own speech and having confidence in it and, through your own physical resources, making it more positive and alive.

Positive and *alive*. Pages of descriptions and definitions of what a good voice is can be summed up in those two words.

IT'S AS EASY AS 1, 2, 3

The foundation for a vibrant, energetic voice is based on the marriage of three factors:

★ good breath support
★ proper pitch
★ a focused, balanced tone.

Good breath support

A well voice is one that is open and reveals the person. It is open to the breath.

Earlier, I mentioned that infants and children breathe naturally and as a result produce free musical voices. As we grow up, the first thing we learn to control is our breath—for example, we hold our breath to gain attention if we don't get our own way, or if we are nervous, angry or upset. This habit of breath inhibition has devastating effects if it is carried through to adulthood. It not only results in creating the habit of upper chest breathing, causing the person to speak with a thin, lifeless tone, it also affects their decision-making power (due to a lack of O_2 to the brain), levels of physical energy and emotional equilibrium. A constant state of physical/mental/emotional imbalance is being supported by these childhood habits.

In my years as a voice teacher, 100 per cent of the people who have walked through my door have all exhibited faulty breathing patterns. Stop for a moment and test yourself. What happens when you take a breath in? I think I know the answer—your upper chest expands and your shoulders rise. When you breathe out, your abdomen expands.

Breathing for speech and health involves breathing in six directions at once. Simply stated, when you breathe in, your mid-section expands, on the breath out it contracts. This is how we naturally breathe when we are asleep, and upon awakening, we put on our clothes of tension and reverse the process—we're back and we're in control! The irony being: we give our control and power away when we breathe incorrectly.

I cannot stress enough the importance of mid-section breath support, not only for the vocal benefits (a full, alive, rich projected sound) but your overall quality of life.

He who half breathes half lives.—Yogic proverb

Proper pitch

Low and husky, thin and weedy, high and whiny, metallic and nasal. Which category is applicable to you? They are all versions of incorrect pitch. When you arise in the morning, you stretch, yawn, wake up your body, shower it, clothe it, feed it. How do you wake up your voice? It usually has to fend for itself and, what's more, be ready and alert for every vocal occasion—for example, bright and breezy, cold and calculating, authoritative and commanding, compassionate and understanding. It's expected to perform these vocal gymnastics 12 to 18 hours a day, *perfectly*, without even a whisper of a warm-up.

Symptoms of voice misuse include tender sore throats, throat clearing, frequent laryngitis, hoarseness, or a voice that tires and fades after a period of speaking. If these symptoms are not corrected, it can lead to irritation of the vocal folds or cords, nodules on polyps, ending in pre-malignancy or cancer of the cords.

Voice health is an essential issue for public speakers, entertainers, telephone salespeople or for anyone who relies on and uses their voice extensively.

A focused, balanced tone

Tone has been described as the music of the voice. A voice with well-produced forward tone vibrates with warmth, energy, colour and richness. It is both pleasant and exciting to the listener. Speakers who possess a compelling tone have the competitive edge. Their voice ignites their audience, giving them the assurance that they *are being listened to*, which is the terminal worry for most speakers.

A focused, balanced tone can be achieved through a blended use of the oral and nasal resonating cavities. The original sound is initiated at the vocal cords and then further vibrates when it comes into contact with the cavities of the throat, nose and mouth. It can be felt as a vibration on a buzzing, tingling, sensation around the nose and the mouth. Ultimately, a balanced tone is dependent upon well-supported breath and correct pitch.

WAKE UP YOUR SOUND

By practising the following 10 exercises you will find your new voice in five minutes a day. Note that these exercises are to be performed in the morning prior to speaking.

Exercise 1: the vacuum exercise

Stand with your feet apart (knees not locked), hands placed on the sides of your ribcage. Exhale all the air out of your lungs and quickly close your mouth and block your nose airway with your thumb and forefinger.

In this position, think of the ribcage expanding forwards and back, side to side.

Resist the need to take a breath for as long as possible. Take the fingers off your nose and keep the mouth firmly closed. Feel the air race in through the nostrils and force the ribcage to expand. Relax and repeat three times.

Exercise 2: sighs and pants

Place one hand on the diaphragm (muscle below the sternum), and feel the mid-section expand on the breath in and contract on the breath out.

* On the exhalation, *sigh* out with a long relaxed Hah sound. Repeat five times.
* Again, on the exhalation, change the sigh to a rapid *pant* with the sound Huh. Repeat five times.
* Alternate each new exhalation with a sigh and a pant.

Exercise 3: the shower routine

Hum in the shower. Hum anything—for example, your name, address, occupation, favourite song (feel the tingling sensation around the nose and lips).

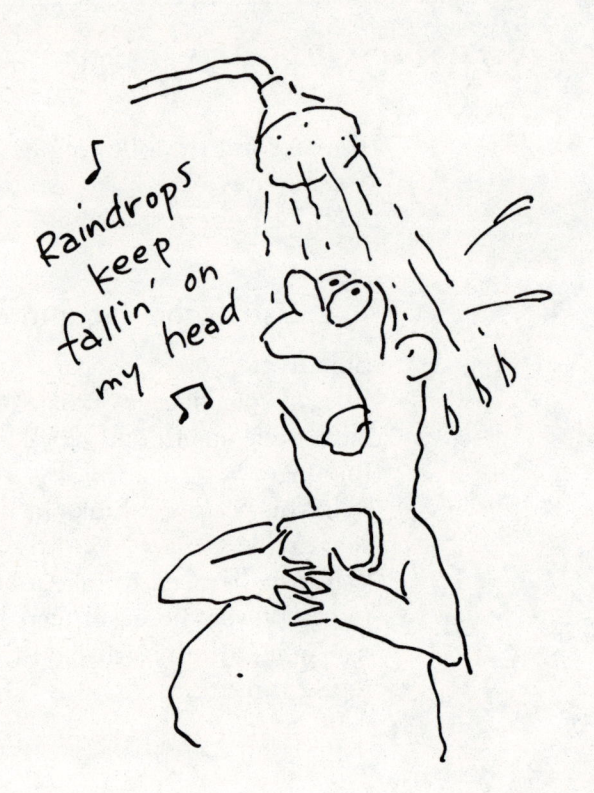

Exercise 4: tap on

Tap rhythmically on the area just below the sternum and continue humming. Change the hum to an Ah sound and continue tapping. Now alternate the Hum and the Ah.

Say your name and address out loud and insert a Hum between each word.

Repeat the above and insert an Ah sound instead of the Hum.

Exercise 5: relaxation

Relax your jaw, lips and tongue by doing the following:

★ *The jaw*. Place the heels of the hands on the hinge of the jaw. Stroke your hands down firmly and smoothly, allowing the jaw to drop freely.
★ *The lips*. Alternate the sounds Wee and Waw. Say them with precision; then increase the speed.
★ *The tongue*. Open your mouth wide, point the tip of your tongue, and then flatten it. Alternate pointing and flattening.

Exercise 6: resonance

Do the following:

* Sit or stand. Tilt the head right back, open the jaw, relax the tongue and place it behind the bottom teeth. In this position, exhale on a warm low continuous Hah sound and direct it to the ceiling. Repeat three times.
* Tilt the head forward into a neutral position. Exhale on a staccato Huh sound and direct it to the wall—for example, Huh, Huh, Huh (exhale in each Huh). The Huh is made with a normal speaking pitch.
* Tilt the head into a downwards position, with the chin pointing towards the chest. Exhale on the Hee sound, making the highest possible sound (it sounds like a mouse on Helium!). It is also a series of short sounds—for example, Hee, Hee, Hee.

Exercise 7: vibration and energy

Make the sound VEE on one continuous note. Continue until you feel the vibration. Repeat with the sound ZEE and the sound GEE. Alternate three times.

Combine VEE, ZEE and GEE with the sounds OO, EE, OH (as in sew)—for example, Voo, Vee, Voh; Goo, Gee, Goh. Repeat five times.

Exercise 8: volume

Place the hand gently over the nose and mouth area. Hum softly, and as you continue, move the hands very slowly away, allowing the sound to change to Ahhhh and to increase in volume until the hands have formed a semi-circle in front of you. Repeat three times.

Exercise 9: clarity

Repeat these words and slowly increase the speed, keeping the words clear and precise:

> Bubble Puddle
> New Union
> Rollalong Wollongong
> Lethal Lather
> Sushi Chef
> Renouf Malouf
> Terrific Frenetic
> Poodle Doodle

Exercise 10: practising your new sound

Read the newspaper, or a book, speak *anything* with an awareness of your new sound. Speak for three minutes with your hand on your diaphragm—reminding you to speak on exhalation.

This is a simple, fast, effective vocal workout. Perform these exercises daily to locate and wake up your sound. The focus should not be in listening for a change, but in feeling the change. Physically feel the vibration and feel and notice the tone of your new voice. Get comfortable and familiar with it. Try it on—wear it with your friends, family and colleagues.

The voice is often at its best when the technical means are forgotten and you are speaking instinctively and responding the words that you are saying.

Remember—your voice is your instrument. Practise it and play it with passion.

IN SUMMARY...

- People assume you are how you sound.
- A dull voice leaves a dull impression.
- A poor voice is reflective of ingrained bad habits. Often the person with a poor self-image speaks with a dead, lifeless tone.
- Symptoms of voice misuse include tender or sore throats, throat clearing, frequent laryngitis, hoarseness, and a voice that tires and fades after a period of speaking.
- A good voice is *positive* and *alive*.
- The foundation for a vibrant, energetic voice is a marriage of three factors: good breath support, proper pitch and a focused, balanced tone.
- A focused, balanced tone (the 'music of the voice') can be achieved through a blended use of the oral and nasal cavities. It depends on well-supported breath and correct pitch.
- Learn and practise the 10 voice exercises to 'wake up your voice'.
- Your voice is your instrument. Practise and play it with passion.

10

PAINTING MENTAL PICTURES

There is one experience from my teenage years that left an indelible impression on me—so much so that I can picture the scene as clearly as if it happened yesterday. I draw upon it time and time again in seminars and public speaking classes. If you've read any of my other books, you may even remember the story of Mrs Fittler's eggs.

This never-to-be-forgotten experience in my life not only serves to make a point about customer service, but also dramatically demonstrates to beginning public speakers how powerful mental images can be.

Before I show you how I use the story to paint vivid mental pictures for my audiences, let me tell you what happened that summer when I was 17...

Every January, Mum and Dad would pack up and head for the old Coogee Bay Hotel in Sydney. They would stay up there while Dad did his buying for the next year from a wholesaler named Hoffnung.

The year I turned 17, they set off for Sydney as usual, leaving a manager in charge of the store. They left me there, too, waiting for my chance to make my first executive decision. After all, I reasoned, I had learned a lot about business just by being there and helping around the shop. I was eager to prove I could handle things just as well as he could—and maybe even better! I was a 17-year-old time bomb, just waiting to explode.

At last my opportunity came. One Tuesday, I was left in charge for a few hours. And every Tuesday for 20 years, Mrs Fittler had come into the store to sell my father a dozen eggs.

Now you must understand that supply and demand had nothing to do with this transaction. It was just something Mrs Fittler did. Every Tuesday she came into town and sold Nicholas Malouf a dozen eggs. So there I was, in charge. And in came Mrs Fittler with her eggs. The eggs were fresh but my relationship with Mrs Fittler was rotten. We had just never got on.

I watched her walk in, her face becoming less friendly when she saw it was that young upstart Doug behind the counter. In that instant I knew what I was going to do. Here was my chance to show who was boss.

She walked up to the counter and held out her package. 'Good morning,' she said. 'Here are your eggs.'

Poor Mrs Fittler. She hadn't realised yet that it was Doug Malouf, the hard-nosed businessman and master negotiator, who she was dealing with this time.

We already had plenty of eggs. I was in a position of strength. So I let her have it right between the eyes.

'We don't want your eggs.'

She didn't seem to notice the crushing blow I'd dealt her. She just fixed me with one unblinking eye.

'Where's your father?' she said. 'He's been buying my eggs for 20 years.'

This was my moment of truth. I had the power to make decisions and I was going to use it.

'My father is in Sydney...and I'm the boss. And we don't need your eggs.'

She looked at me again without any signs of emotion. She still didn't seem to realise that I'd won.

'Is that your final word?'

'Yes,' I said.

My cousin Betty in accounts had been watching what was happening. I looked across at her, expecting to see a new respect on her face for my decisive action. Instead, she was smiling at me. But it wasn't a triumphant sort of smile. It was more...pitying.

Mrs Fittler walked across to her.

'Betty, I'd like you to make up my account...and the Cassidy's, and the Jarriday's and all the other Fittler accounts. It'll save them a trip.'

Have you got any idea of what it's like to be 17 and to have just cost your father's business its best five accounts...plus another six that weren't bad either? Believe me, a wisdom tooth extraction without anaesthetic looks attractive by comparison.

Suicide becomes a genuine option.

Mrs Fittler clearly didn't understand the laws of supply and demand. She didn't notice that I was in a position of negotiating strength.

She just closed 11 accounts and left the store.

Betty was very supportive.

'Just wait till your father gets back,' she said. 'He'll kill you.'

Actually, he didn't kill me. He was very understanding. He discussed the matter calmly, and outlined the options available to me.

'Get the accounts back,' he said, 'or don't bother to come home.'

When I got off my bike and walked up to Mrs Fittler's front door, there she was, framed in the doorway. The theme from *High Noon* filled the room behind her. Things didn't look good. I didn't have to open my mouth.

'Your father sent you, didn't he?'

I nodded.

'Let me tell you something, son. I'm coming back to your father's store. But it's only because he's such a good man. I wouldn't want to hurt him because he's got a fool for a son.'

What could I say?

'There are the eggs,' she said.

She was right. The eggs were there. The same eggs she'd brought in three weeks ago. Wrapped in the same newspaper. You didn't need to be able to see them to know they were there.

I took a long look at them.

'Well, make up your mind,' she said. 'Do you want them or not?'

She had me, and she knew it. The master negotiator had been beaten. I picked them up delicately, and turned to go. She put her hand on my arm to stop me and handed me another parcel.

'Here's two dozen more for the last two weeks. Make sure your father gets them…all of them.'

When I got home from Mrs Fittler's, my father underlined the lesson I had learnt. 'Always remember that the customer is your business,' he said, disposing of the eggs. 'The moment you stop giving customer service is the moment you don't have a business.'

You see, what I hadn't understood was that buying Mrs Fittler's eggs was not a business transaction. That purchase showed that Dad wasn't just a shopkeeper. He was a part of the community, giving as well as taking. Those eggs represented the relationship of mutual trust and respect he shared with all his customers.

So that's what I learnt. Trust is the basis for prosperity in business. If your customers trust you they won't be one sale wonders. They'll keep coming back. And they'll bring their friends.

What happened to me might be excusable because I was only 17. And it is easy to be wise about it 30 years later. But I still see business people behaving in much the same way in their contacts with their clients. So remember to keep your eyes open for Mrs Fittler. Sooner or later she's going to walk into your office. And when she does, be sure that you buy her eggs.

I use the story of Mrs Fittler's eggs to show people how they can take an incident from life and make it live for an audience. It's a great story to tell from the front, because it's on me. It doesn't bring in race, sex or creed. When I tell it, I point the finger only at myself, and that means the material is *safe*.

Why is this storytelling technique so effective?

For one thing, when you are drawing from your own experience, you don't need notes or props—you can 'chat it'. The blueprint of that experience is so strong and so vivid in your own mind that it's easy to bring it to life for an audience.

Aim to build a store of stories from the host of experiences in your life. What lessons have you learnt in life? Most of us can remember at least one. Who or what taught you that lesson? Can you turn it into a story by carefully choosing words and images that will speak directly to the cameras in people's minds?

Learn to embellish your story so that your audience can vividly imagine it with you, as I did with the story of Mrs Fittler's eggs. Select words that will appeal to the five senses: sight, touch, taste, smell and hearing.

For example, when retelling the story, instead of simply saying 'a dozen eggs', I might say something like: 'I can still see the eggs, wrapped up in their newspaper on Mrs Fittler's table.' What can you picture more easily? 'A dozen eggs' or 'eggs wrapped up in newspaper on a table'? Those words were chosen specifically to help the listener picture what they looked like.

Here are some more examples from the same story:

* *Smell:* 'You didn't have to see them to know they were there.'
* *Hearing:* 'The theme from *High Noon* filled the room behind her.'
* *Touch:* 'She put her hand on my arm to stop me.' (Here, become an actor. Actually play the part of two different people—Mrs Fittler, reaching out to put her hand on your arm. Then turn, glance down at your arm and look at the space opposite you as though you could really see Mrs Fittler standing there while you mimic the conversation. Dramatise it! Exaggerate it! Be an actor. If you behave as though that person is actually there with you, the audience will be able to 'see' them too.)

See how it works? You were there. The members of your audience were not. So you have to help them draw those vivid mental pictures.

Don't forget that pacing is a very important part of helping people to picture a scene. Just as variations in pace in a passage of music enhance the enjoyment of the listener, strategic pauses will build suspense and add power to a punchline. For example:

> Betty was very supportive (pause)...'Just wait till your father gets back,' she said. 'He'll kill you.' (Act it out! Point your finger when you are playing Betty. Let your face express your emotions.)

> Actually, he didn't kill me. He was very understanding. He discussed the matter calmly, and outlined the options available to me (pause)...'Get the accounts back,' he said, 'or don't bother to come home.'

Similarly, when you are using an emotional event as a basis for your story, you can increase the impact of your words by speaking more quietly, or by using pauses. Try *increasing* the volume when describing *dramatic* confrontations. In short, experiment with different storytelling techniques, and expressive words and phrases, until you find a style that's right for you.

WHAT MAKES A GOOD STORY?

To get more of an understanding about what constitutes a good story, cast your mind back to childhood. Back to a time when you listened entranced to a story that carried you away, to a different time or place. It may have been a bedtime story, read while you were tucked up safely in crisp sheets and warm blankets. Perhaps you lay there, fighting off sleep, because you simply had to find out what happened next. What would happen to the Darling children, when they left their safe home to fly with Peter Pan to The Land of Lost Boys? Would they fall out of the sky? Would they be able to find their way back?

Or perhaps you've tapped a memory of a warm day in the classroom, the heat of summer settling like a heavy blanket over the room, while your teacher read to the class from an open book. You can remember sitting there slumped over a hard wooden desk, only vaguely aware of voices from the classroom next door and of the fly buzzing at the window pane, because you are listening so hard, not wanting to miss a word.

Some of you might remember instead listening to exciting stories about family dramas, exchanged over cups of coffee at the kitchen table. Did you sit there enthralled, trying to be as quiet as a mouse so no one would order you out to play?

Whatever comes to mind when you think of those stories that were so full of colour and drama that you found yourself holding your breath in anticipation of the outcome, you can be sure all those tales had one thing in common:

Vivid mental pictures.

And that is one of the secrets of the great communicators. They are able to paint mental scenes for us with such clarity that we are able to imagine every tiny detail. We sit, unconsciously leaning forward a little, picturing the setting and the people in the story.

We are hooked.

This skill of painting vivid mental pictures can be learned. Any one of you can, with practice, have *your* audience waiting with bated breath for your next word. That need to know 'what happened next' is what I rely on when I tell the story of Mrs Fittler's eggs.

Part of the power of learning to paint mental pictures is that the process imprints the story in *your* mind. When a scene comes alive for you, it will come alive for your listeners. If you watch the world's best speakers, you'll see that they are unbelievably good at telling stories. They draw the listeners into their world with the same skill that best-selling authors use to hook their readers.

Sometimes, people pick up a book intending to 'just finish the chapter'. Famous last words! They end up reading until the small hours of the morning, barely noticing time passing—because the writer has switched on the film projector in their minds, and introduced them to a new world full of colour and light and drama.

You can do the same thing. Switch on that film projector in your listener's minds, through your skill at painting mental pictures.

PRACTISING PAINTING MENTAL PICTURES

Try these exercises to improve your skills at painting mental pictures.

The orange

Using the five senses, describe an orange.

A childhood experience

Describe a childhood experience and bring it to life by painting pictures from the child's point of view. (People look very large...loud noises are extra scary...crossing the bedroom in the dark...being treated as though you were deaf, dumb and blind by adults...joy in small things...etc.)

Your teenage years

Tell a story about your teenage years, making every effort to bring it to life by referring to songs and/or movies of that era, crazy things you used to do, worries about fitting in and being accepted.

I remember...

Begin an anecdote with 'I remember...' one big event, or lots of small memories. Jot down the specific things that bring that memory to life.

The emotions

Work your way through the emotions. Write down as many as you can think of, then describe them: 'love is...'; 'hate is...'; 'embarrassment is...'; 'fear is...'; 'joy is...'; 'anxiety is...'; and so on. You will find that when you try to explain what these feelings are, scenes will come to mind. Describe those scenes in vivid detail. Make us feel the fear, blush with embarrassment, worry along with you.

One of my favourite things...

Begin a story with 'One of my favourite things...' Describe this 'thing' or activity in such vivid detail that we wish we could share it with you.

I learned a lesson from...

Begin a story with 'I learned a lesson from...' Many speakers have a store of anecdotes that they draw upon to illustrate a certain point. What lessons have you learned in life? What taught you those lessons? Jot down anything that comes to mind—serious, funny, tongue in cheek, sad.

I grew up when...

Begin a story with 'I grew up when...' Can you think of a turning point in your life? An event that suddenly made you see the world from an adult's point of view? What happened? Bring it to life for us.

Imitate another person

Study the way people speak. Being able to tell a tale imitating someone's speech patterns often makes it more dramatic. Look for key words or patterns in people's speech rather than dialect. It's hard to carry off different accents. Think of someone you know well and try to write a paragraph just as they would speak. Mentally 'listen' to them speaking as you do so.

A dramatic hook

The 'hook', or the beginning of your speech, is most important. It's often here that you either capture or lose your listeners. Write a dramatic 'hook' that will have your audience listening with bated breath for the next sentence.

IN SUMMARY...

* To keep the attention of your audience, take an incident from life and make it live. In other words, become a skilful *storyteller*.
* Build a store of stories from the host of experiences in your life.
* Learn to embellish your story so the audience can vividly imagine the setting and the action. Select words that will appeal to the five senses: sight, touch, taste, smell and hearing.

11

COMMON PROBLEMS AND PRACTICAL SOLUTIONS

After two decades of public speaking and teaching others about public speaking, I now have a pretty clear idea of the areas in which the novice public speaker is most likely to run into trouble. This chapter is to make you aware of them before you start, and thus prepare you to deal with them.

THE PROBLEM: POOR PREPARATION

It will come as no surprise to you that this is the first point! I'm sure you have had to suffer on occasion from a speaker who is ill-prepared. Your feelings are likely to be anything from anger at having to sit there and listen, to squirming with embarrassment because the speaker is making such a hash of things.

It's desirable that you should know more about your subject than *most* people in the audience. So if you don't want to spend days buried in research at the library, it makes sense to speak only about:

✭ what you know
✭ what you can easily find out.

The solution

Research and preparation are essential. You have to understand a subject properly before you can hope to share your knowledge and understanding with other people.

You should not be a speaker in search of a topic. Your speaking should grow naturally out of *who you are*, *what you have done* or *what you already know*.

Even if you know the subject well, don't feel that you can cut down on preparation. You might know your subject very well. You might have a filing cabinet full of prepared speeches. But *don't* settle for pulling out a script that is 'close enough' to a set topic. You have to prepare for the exact subject and specific audience involved. Continuing research keeps you alive as a speaker.

Remember that research isn't something done exclusively in libraries. It should involve a number of information-collecting activities. You might:

✭ Draw on your unique knowledge and experience on the subject.
✭ Read about it, looking especially for information that will help you add interest to your presentation.
✭ Ask an expert—that is, people with special knowledge of the subject—to help you.

Dr Ken McFarlane, a truly gifted speaker, has said that:

> ...the truth behind every spectacular presentation is heaps of unspectacular preparation.

Make this true of your speeches.

THE PROBLEM: MATERIAL NOT SUITED TO THE AUDIENCE

You start speaking...and somewhere along the line you realise you've lost them. You have misjudged your audience; you're not giving them what they want.

The solution

Find out as much as possible about your audience before you start preparing your speech. For them to be gathered there in one place to listen to you speak, they must have *something* in common. Find out what it is, and use that information in designing your speech. Ask:

* What type of people are they? (Students? Politicians? Priests? Gardeners?)
* What do they expect from me? (Information? Inspiration? Ideas for action?)

When you answer these questions, you can start narrowing things down even more:

* Will they be interested in my subject?
* Will I be able to offer them anything that they can use?

Imagine this scenario: A friend of yours has just returned from overseas. A week after the 'hello, I'm home!' call comes the dreaded invitation to come around and watch the 2000 slides and six home videos they've taken. You can't get out of it without mortally offending your bosom buddy.

The night comes. After the first five slides you sink hopelessly into the lounge and think: 'only 1995 to go...'

Let's change the scene. (That's the good thing about imagined situations: one blink and you've conjured up a totally different story.) Suppose your friend rings up and says: 'We're back! Didn't you say you're going to Hong Kong later this year? We've got slides here that show the best hotels—and the *worst*. And some others that show where we got the best discounts. Want to come around and have a look?'

You agree enthusiastically and head off out the door.

What can we learn from this?

The first person has their attention firmly fixed on their own needs and interests. They need to tell their friends all about the trip they found so fascinating, so they show and tell them everything.

The second person has shaped their presentation to fit the interests of their friends—and they offer them potentially useful information.

As a speaker you have to do the same thing. From the mass of information you could use, select the facts that seem most likely to interest, entertain and inform your audience.

THE PROBLEM: FAILURE TO PRACTISE A SPEECH

There are plenty of speakers out there who have gone along to a speaking engagement full of confidence and well-versed in their subject matter, only to find that the words do not flow smoothly. Reason? *Lack of practice*.

The solution

We don't need to say too much on this point, since we discussed the importance of practice in some detail in Chapter 8. So just remember: it's only when you practise the actual delivery that you discover the differences between writing an essay and writing for the spoken word. Sentences that look beautiful on paper often prove to be impossible to speak—they're too long, or they prove to be tongue-twisters, or they sound impossibly stuffy. Practice will help to eliminate these problems.

THE PROBLEM: FAILURE TO SPEAK TO TIME

Sometimes you will be able to suggest the amount of time you need to get the message across. In many cases, however, the time will be set for you. Your audience knows how long you're supposed to speak from the program; the organisers have planned their agenda around your speaking for a set length of time. Therefore:

★ If you speak for significantly less time than expected, they:
   — may doubt *your* knowledge and authority on the subject
   — will be considerably put out by having to think fast and 'fill in'.

★ If you speak for significantly longer than expected they:
   — may become bored/annoyed/restless
   — will be considerably put out by having to cut down time for other sections of the program (or even worse, cut down time for lunch).

The solution

Clearly establish the length of time you are expected to speak, plan your speech to suit the time and *stick to it*.

THE PROBLEM: INFORMATION OVERLOAD

Experts in any field have a tendency to want to tell everything they know. In a speech, this is a road to certain disaster. The effective speaker knows that there are limits to what an audience can absorb in any given period of time.

The solution

You should write down in a single sentence the basic message you want to get across. Then select three to five major points that will help you get that message through to your audience effectively. Three to five ideas is about right for a 20-minute speech.

Here is a handy basic format:

1. Tell them what you are going to say.
2. Say the same thing in an elaborated form.
3. Find illustrations to make your ideas concrete.
4. Tell them the same thing in a different way using an analogy.

Speakers shouldn't choke their audiences with knowledge. They should present a limited number of bite-sized pieces of information that can be easily digested and properly appreciated.

THE PROBLEM: TOO MUCH JARGON

Sometimes it seems that the world we live in couldn't operate without acronyms, archaic language and techno-talk. To the hapless listener, some speeches might as well be in Martian.

If you use terminology and words that the audience can't understand, they'll not only switch off, they'll feel like hurling rotten fruit.

The solution

Try the following:

1. Don't use acronyms or abbreviations unless you explain what they mean.
2. Use simple, powerful words.
3. Explain technical information or statistics with examples that are familiar to most people.

For example, on a recent interstate flight, just as dinner was being served, the captain announced that we were flying at an altitude of some 33 000 feet. That meant nothing to me. I can't grasp the meaning of an altitude that high. I only know it's a long way to fall.

Having made that announcement, however, he went on to say that it was 10 kilometres, or the distance from Sydney to Watson's Bay. I could instantly grasp the concept.

This is what you need to do as a speaker. Relate what you are saying to ideas and events that are familiar to the listener. Forget the jargon. Use simple words and analogies drawn from the common experience of ordinary people. Then you can be sure they'll be understood.

THE PROBLEM: LACK OF EYE CONTACT

Many people look at the ceiling as if their cue cards were stuck to it. By doing that, they are breaking one of the basic rules of human communication: if you want the person to whom you're speaking to listen to you, you look at them.

Speaking to a group is no different. Don't look up, don't look down, look at them from the start.

The solution

Practise regular glances at each section of the room. If you are close enough, choose a few people with whom you can hold eye contact for a few seconds at the end of a sentence every now and again. You'll be amazed at the difference it makes to the audience's attention.

If you are using notes and need to look at them to refresh your memory: pause, look at your notes, and then raise your eyes deliberately to look at your audience before you begin speaking again.

THE PROBLEM: SPEAKING AT THE WRONG SPEED

Your audience needs time to think about what you are saying. But if you are spraying words around like water from a garden hose, many of your points will be lost. So *slow down*! It's mainly the fear of facing an audience that prompts speakers to make their delivery too quickly.

On the other hand, some speakers are much too deliberate in their delivery. Slowing down is a good idea, but slow down *too* much and you might have to go around waking up your audience.

The solution
There are three ways to regulate your pace:

* Use a cassette recorder to check your pace. It will be quite obvious if you are speaking too slowly or too quickly.
* Learn to pace yourself by observing audience responses to your speech. If they laugh, pause. Let the laughter sink in. Learn to use the power of the pause. Then pick up the momentum of your presentation again.
* Use a metronome: I can almost see you frown at this one! Aren't metronomes for musicians? Yes, they are—but they're also ideal for helping beginning speakers! It makes a lot of sense when you think about what a metronome actually does. It helps the musician to keep to a specified pace—and that's just as important in public speaking as it is in playing music. (For the non-musical reader: a metronome is a handy little gadget you can buy at a musical supplies store. You simply set it so that it starts ticking to a regular beat.) Set your metronome to a slow pace, and modify the pace of your delivery to keep time with it. Every so often, pause for a couple of beats for effect. Works like a charm!

THE PROBLEM: LACK OF ENTHUSIASM

The old saying is pretty true:

> *There are no boring subjects. There are just boring speakers.*

If you don't seem very interested in what you are saying you can hardly expect to hold the attention of the audience.

The solution
Try the following:

* Use your voice expressively. Let it reflect your enthusiasm for your subject.
* Use gestures to show your commitment to your point of view, and to emphasise your key points.

- ✶ Speak with conviction. Let them feel your energy and conviction through your voice.
- ✶ Keep it moving. The audience will make up its mind about you in the first few minutes. So punch it to them. Keep up the pace. If you want people to buy your ideas you must present them with gusto.
- ✶ Humour is important too. People want to enjoy what you have to say. Be warm; look directly at those friendly faces; use humour to invite them to share your enjoyment of your subject.

When you speak, you use your personality to project your subject. This becomes easier if you work on showing interest and enthusiasm in all your daily contacts with other people. If you succeed in doing that you will naturally convey the same qualities in your public presentations.

THE PROBLEM: POOR PRESENTATION SKILLS

It's a shame to let good material and careful preparation be spoilt by poor presentation skills. There are two main problems with most poor presentations:

- ✶ distracting body language
- ✶ distracting verbal language.

The solution

Use what the experts call the *three Vs of presentation*:

1. Visual aspects of communication—What they see you do.
2. Verbal aspects of communication—What they hear you say.
3. Vocal aspects of communication—How they hear you say it.

NON-VERBAL (e.g. facial expressions, gestures)

55%

INTONATION, STRESS AND SPEED
(how it is said)

38%

WORDS, WORDS, WORDS (what is said)

7%

Each of these aspects of your presentation should work together to make your message clear and interesting. But if they are in competition with each other, the visual factors tend to overwhelm the rest.

Nerves can cause us to rock and roll and twitch; to take our glasses on and off; to play with coins in our pockets; to sway unsteadily; to stand rigidly; to turn monotonously from one side of the audience to the other.

Any of these habits can destroy the impact of any speech. However, to control distracting habits you have to be aware of them. So seek the help of friends. And don't get upset when they tell you the truth!

Make sure you stand up straight. Remember that looking confident is more than half of *being* confident. Let your audience know that you expect to succeed.

Distracting verbal habits include:

✯ frequently repeated phrases like 'um', 'er', 'right', 'you know'.
✯ colourless, monotonous speech
✯ unclear speech—too fast, too slow, poorly articulated.

Again, use a cassette recorder or a friend to help you pinpoint the difficulties.

You are unlikely to find that you are doing all of these things wrong! It's probably only one or two that are causing you problems. Look at yourself honestly, choose to do something about the problems, and go on positively from there. You have achieved a lot to get this far!

GOOD LUCK OR GOOD PLANNING?

The following '7 Rs to Successful Speaking' will help you overcome many of the problems highlighted in this chapter. The 7 Rs also bring together many of the key ideas emphasised throughout *How to be the Best Speaker in Town*. Remember:

Good luck is mainly due to careful planning.

Common Problems and Practical Solutions

THE '7 RS TO SUCCESSFUL SPEAKING'

1. *Research it.* Find out as much as you can about the subject—read—discuss—interview experts—watch films.

2. *Reduce it to paper.* Writing it out will help you select from among the facts you have discovered. Try writing a one-sentence summary of your message.

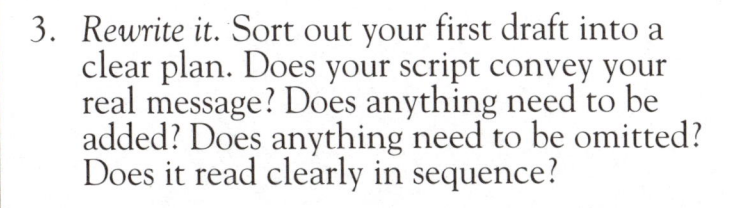

3. *Rewrite it.* Sort out your first draft into a clear plan. Does your script convey your real message? Does anything need to be added? Does anything need to be omitted? Does it read clearly in sequence?

4. *Re-read it.* Read it aloud as well as silently. Does it make sense? Is it too long? Is it too short? By reading aloud you get a feel for your own material. Now edit and tighten the script.

Continued…

5. *Rehearse it*. Try it out on a friend. Test the reaction. Do they like it? Full rehearsal ensures success. The wrinkles are ironed out. The nerves are soothed by repetition.

6. *Reduce it to key words*. Read through the full script. Select the key words—the ones that will help you recall what you have written. Write the key words down on cards or in a notebook. Don't use a typed sheet.

7. *Rip it up*. If you've prepared it carefully enough and rehearsed it often enough, you'll have it in your head. Throw it away.

IN SUMMARY...

* You must understand a subject properly before you can hope to share your knowledge and understanding with other people.
* Research involves:
    — drawing on your own knowledge and experience
    — reading
    — viewing and listening to audio-visual resources
    — talking to others.
* *'Behind every spectacular presentation is heaps of unspectacular preparation.'* (Dr Ken McFarlane).
* Clearly establish the length of time you are expected to speak; plan your speech to suit the time, and *stick to it*.
* Speakers should present listeners with a limited number of bite-sized pieces of information that can be easily digested and properly appreciated.
* Don't use acronyms or abbreviations unless you explain what they mean.
* Use simple, powerful words.
* Use examples that people will find familiar to explain technical information or statistics.
* Make eye contact: practise regular glances at each section of the room.
* Learn to regulate your pace: not too fast, not too slow.
* To prevent audience boredom, use your voice expressively, use gestures, speak with conviction, and keep up the pace.
* Don't use distracting body language or phrases ('you know' or 'what I mean is...')
* Master the three Vs of presentation: the Visual, Vocal and Verbal aspects.
* Master the '7 Rs of Successful Speaking': Research it, Reduce it to paper; Rewrite it; Re-read it; Rehearse it; Reduce it to key words; and then Rip it up!

12

YOUR SELF-IMPROVEMENT PROGRAM

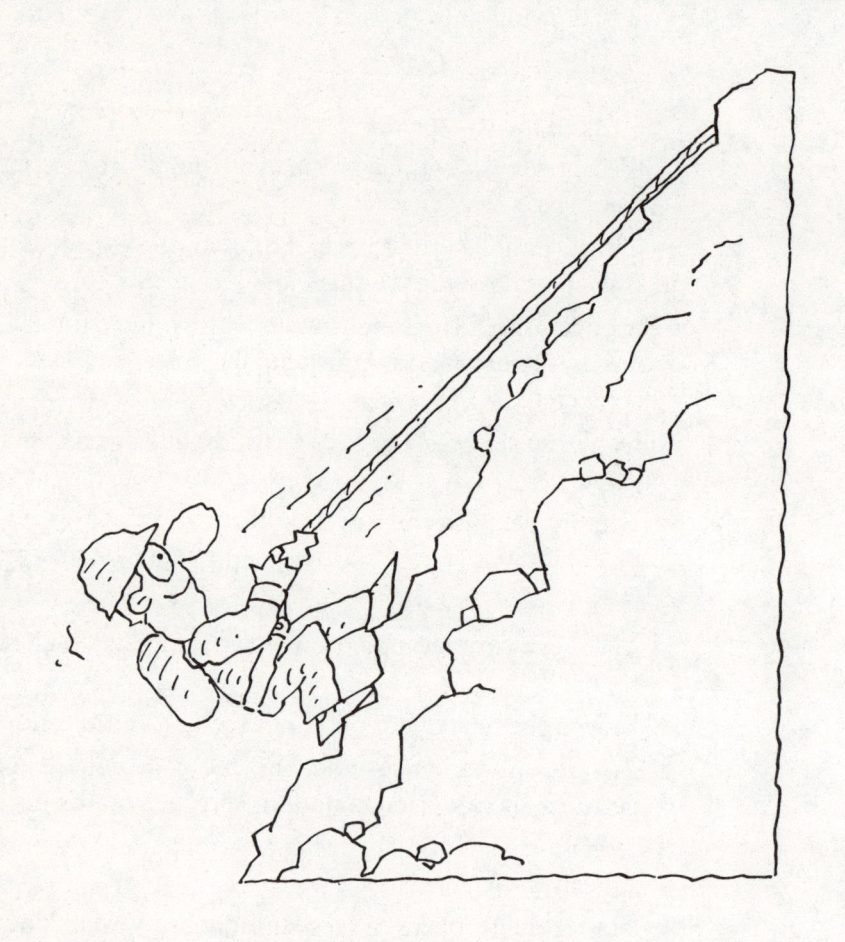

THE STEPS TO SELF-IMPROVEMENT

Only you know where you are in the development of your public speaking skills. So only you know the best place to start on this program. You may not find it necessary to start right at the beginning, if you have already had a little speaking experience. It could be that you are strong in some areas but need to practise others. (For example, you may know how to put together a good speech, but need practice with the delivery.)

If you are new to public speaking, you will find that the Self-Improvement Program provides you with a handy step-by-step guide to help you develop and hone your skills.

Step 1: practise every day

You will find it a lot easier to develop skills in effective public speaking if you practise the basics in everyday conversation. If you practise using colourful, expressive language, if you work on your listening skills, and if you learn to 'read' the other person's reactions as you speak, you will find that it is reflected by your success when you speak to larger groups. So the first step in your Self-Improvement Program will cover those three things.

Use colourful, expressive language

The following hints will help you improve your use of colourful, expressive language:

* Practise using strong verbs to illustrate what you have to say. For example, not 'He walked in my direction, looking angry' but 'He strode towards me, and I had a feeling I wasn't going to like what he had to say.' The use of the word 'strode' gives the listener a clearer picture of how you were approached. In addition, 'I had a feeling I wasn't going to like what he had to say' lets them imagine the look of anger on his face without your having to tell them. It works better than 'looking angry' because they have to work (but not too hard) to make that extra connection, which involves them more with the speech.
* Keep a notebook of useful words, phrases and techniques. When you hear other people using words and expressions that conjure up vivid images for you, make a note of them. Could you use the same expressions? How did they manage the effect they achieved?
* Make a conscious effort to entertain family and friends by making your stories interesting. (You don't have to be a comedian to entertain.) Learn to express yourself so well that they look forward to anecdotes about your work or social life. Expressive language involves the use of clever pacing and timing, as well as the use of interesting words.

- To understand timing, watch some of the popular sitcoms (situation comedies) on television. Everyone will have different tastes, but most of us can find one we like. How do the actors achieve their effects? Some of it is visual, while some is through the words, pacing and timing. Try to identify what it is that makes a line effective. (You are not necessarily doing this to learn how to be a comedian, although if you are naturally witty this could be a possibility. You are looking at pacing and timing related to the choice of words.)

Work on your listening skills

Practise your listening skills by trying to empathise with the other person (or persons) as much as possible. Forget about the interesting story you have to tell. Concentrate on the other person. React only to what they say, and the emotions behind what they say. Remember:

- listen
- identify (in your mind) what their message is
- respond to what they say in a way that makes it clear that you understand that message
- give them cues that encourage them to keep talking.

By mastering listening skills in a one-to-one situation or a small group, you begin to understand a lot more about other people's needs and concerns. This helps when you later have to think about what your audience might want from you. But listening is only a part of the 'response' package. Learning to 'read' the other person is an essential part of communication.

Learn to 'read' other people

There's plenty of material around on people's personal styles and how to read them. Look for books in this area if you want to know more. Meanwhile, there are certain clues that will set you on the way:

- Does the person you're talking to speak in a slow, relaxed manner or use a faster, staccato delivery?
- Do they use plenty of eye contact, or just glance occasionally at the other person?

- Listen to the way they use language. Do they have pet words and phrases? Do they have a casual style, with a lot of the interpretation left up to the listener, or do they prefer a more formal approach?
- Does their speech indicate they are heavily influenced by television, current music, current films, or current gossip about people in the public eye?
- Does their body language (facial expressions, open/closed stance, eye contact or lack of it) indicate that they are interested in what you have to say?
- Try the 'mirroring' technique: make your body language, facial expressions and language style 'mirror' that of the person with whom you are speaking. (This doesn't mean being a carbon copy! Rather, you should try to reflect their general style, so they feel you can identify with them.)

If you become accustomed to 'reading' people as you interact with them on a daily basis, you will move smoothly into being able to read an audience in the same way. Although you won't be talking to them, you will become adept at picking up other cues that will warn you if you need to adapt your presentation as you go.

Step 2: seek out opportunities

In the beginning stages of public speaking, you should seek out opportunities for making short speeches or presentations. You should also look for opportunities to practise in a supportive atmosphere.

Public speaking clubs and courses

Inquire about clubs such as Toastmasters and ITC (International Training in Communication) that exist to help people develop their public speaking skills. These offer the opportunity to build your skills through a series of short speeches that will be evaluated in a friendly, supportive atmosphere by experienced club members. You can move at your own pace.

Commercial courses might be preferable for those who want to learn quickly. Most such courses run from one day to six weeks.

Opportunities at your place of work

The workplace offers many opportunities to brush up on your speaking skills.

* Look for opportunities to speak at meetings, or offer to head committees.
* If management is looking for volunteers to represent the company at seminars or to speak briefly to community groups, put your hand up.
* If the opportunity comes up, offer to go on a panel to answer questions about your area of expertise. This panel might be at a convention, or at a staff meeting. Panels are an excellent way to start speaking in public, because you don't have to write a speech—you're just answering questions or giving your opinion, and there are other people there to support you. Just make sure you know your stuff!

Opportunities outside the workplace

Clubs and committees of all kinds will give you opportunities to speak. You can talk about fund-raising (or whatever is relevant) to your Parents and Citizens Group at your children's schools; you can talk to clubs (such as View or Rotary) about your career, hobbies or interests; you can volunteer to teach a new skill to your craft group.

Step 3: speak on appropriate topics

Most effective speakers don't try to be all things to all people. They speak on topics that are of particular interest to them. Don't agree to speak on a topic simply because it suits the person asking you. You're the one who has to give the speech! Make sure you feel comfortable about the topic.

What will you speak on?

List your areas of expertise, your hobbies and your interests. Agree to give speeches based on this list.

Start a speech file

Try the following:

* Clip and file interesting magazine and newspaper articles.
* Jot down ideas as they occur to you, and start collecting interesting anecdotes of your own. Write out anecdotes briefly as things happen to you or as you hear about them, and file under the appropriate topic.
* File 'old' speeches under subject headings.

Step 4: determine what's in it for the audience

Before you start to write any speech, ask yourself *who* the audience is and *what* they want to hear from you. Then follow this procedure each time:

Writing a speech

Use these steps:

* Brainstorm for ideas. Ask yourself:

    What points am I going to make? How am I going to make them?

    Sort ideas into an introduction, body and conclusion.
* Write an interesting beginning using the ABC formula.
* Keep the body of your speech simple, and look for ways to identify with the audience.
* End on a positive note.
* Edit your speech so it flows naturally when you speak.
* Reduce your speech to key words and phrases.

Writing a script

If you are going to write a script, remember it should not look like an essay! Refer to the chapter on script writing (Chapter 6), and:

* Practise skim reading and making eye contact.
* Use a large typeface and use slash marks to indicate pauses.
* Rehearse, rehearse, rehearse.
* Emphasise: clarity, simplicity, words that conjure up pictures in the minds of the audience, and different ways of repeating ideas.

Step 5: work on your delivery

Assuming that you can speak with confidence on your chosen topic and you have prepared a good script, you need to work on the *delivery* of your speech.

* Practise the delivery of your speech until you feel completely comfortable and familiar with the material.
* Work either from a script prepared for reading aloud or from key words or phrases.

- ★ Practise speaking over noise.
- ★ Keep a practise log book to 'keep yourself honest' and to record your progress.

Get feedback from others and from listening to a tape:

Your words

- ★ Do you sound likeable and interesting?
- ★ Are any sentences/words/anecdotes too long?
- ★ Do the ideas and points made flow on logically? Are there any flaws in your reasoning?
- ★ Is the speech relevant to the audience and/or conference theme?
- ★ How does your voice sound? Too high, fast, slow? Is there an upward inflection at the end of sentences?
- ★ If you use humour, does the timing work?
- ★ Does the speech need tightening up (for example, rambling stories, too much repetition of ideas)? Do any sections need to be cut? Do you need to rewrite anything that is slow or uninteresting? How would you say it to a friend?

Your voice

- ★ Does your voice sound natural? Are you projecting your voice properly?
- ★ Would speech exercises be beneficial to you?

Timing

- ★ Do you need to slow down?
- ★ Are you breathing normally or holding your breath—or gasping for breath?
- ★ If you are using humour, have you got the timing right? (Ask for feedback.)

Gestures and stance

- Have you identified any annoying habits (for example, fidgeting, saying 'you know' at the end of sentences, nervous twitches, slipping glasses on and off)?
- Do you use hand gestures effectively—that is, no small, fussy gestures.

Step 6: monitor your progress

As you deliver more speeches, continue to fine-tune your technique by monitoring your progress.

- Record (audio or video tape) as many speeches as you can.
- Continue to ask for feedback from friends and other speakers.
- If the organisers are handing out evaluation sheets, ask if you can see how you rated—or sometimes, hand out your own. Ask for feedback on how interesting/entertaining/useful the audience found your presentation.
- Write down your own feelings about your delivery and insights about what does or doesn't work.
- Push yourself to search for new challenges by joining advanced speakers' associations or volunteering for presentations a step beyond your comfort zone.

Step 7: become a mentor

The final step that will add the gloss to your speaking career is to help others along the path and make the learning process a little easier for them. Teaching a skill builds your understanding as well as giving something back.

- Evaluate the performance of others and show them how to improve their performance.
- Look for opportunities to help others gain self-confidence—volunteer to train others in the workplace in speaking skills; become a mentor to one or two up-and-coming speakers.

SELF-IMPROVEMENT PROGRESS LOG

Step 1: practise every day

AREA FOR IMPROVEMENT	ACTIVITIES
Use of colourful and expressive language	❑ I have established a personal notebook to jot down words and expressions that work for me. ❑ I have practised using strong verbs in anecdotes. ❑ I have practised 'entertaining' family and friends with anecdotes on 1 2 3 4 5 6 7 8 9 10 11 12 occasions (cross these off on each occasion). ❑ I have watched TV sitcoms and made notes about pacing and timing.
Listening skills	❑ I have practised using listening skills on 1 2 3 4 5 6 7 8 9 10 11 12 occasions and made notes about what I discovered.
Learning to 'read' other people	❑ I have made notes on the 'personal styles' of the people I meet. ❑ I have tried the 'mirroring' technique and made notes on the results.

Step 2: seek out opportunities

AREA FOR IMPROVEMENT	ACTIVITIES
Public speaking clubs and courses	❑ I have enrolled in a public speaking club. ❑ I have enrolled in a public speaking course.
Opportunities at your place of work	❑ I have made a presentation at a meeting. ❑ I have made a short presentation or given a short talk while representing the company. ❑ I have sat on a panel and responded to questions.
Opportunities outside the workplace	❑ I have spoken to a group at a school. ❑ I have spoken to a community club (such as Rotary). ❑ I have volunteered to teach a skill to a group of some kind.

Step 3: speak on appropriate topics

AREA FOR IMPROVEMENT	ACTIVITIES
What will you speak on?	❏ I have listed my areas of expertise, my interests and my hobbies.
Start a speech file	❏ I have begun a speech file under appropriate headings. ❏ I have written out several anecdotes that I could use and filed them appropriately. ❏ I have filed any old speeches. ❏ I have started clipping and filing interesting articles.

Step 4: determine what's in it for the audience

AREA FOR IMPROVEMENT	ACTION
Writing a speech	❏ For each speech, I first ask who the audience is and what they want to hear. ❏ I follow the procedure of brainstorming, and sorting my ideas into an introduction, body and conclusion. ❏ I have used suitable anecdotes to illustrate a point. ❏ I spend time constructing an interesting beginning and a positive ending, and conclude by reminding the audience of my main message or key points. ❏ Each speech has a balance between stories, facts, statistics, examples and information. ❏ I have let the audience know what's in it for them. ❏ I know how to edit the speech and reduce it to key words and phrases.
Writing a script	❏ I have practised 'skim reading' and making eye contact with speeches and newspaper articles. ❏ I have rehearsed reading from a script until it sounds as natural as speaking to someone. ❏ I have eliminated all awkward phrases and over-long sentences.

Step 5: work on your delivery

AREA FOR IMPROVEMENT	ACTION
Feedback: — on flow of speech and word usage — on sound of voice — on timing — on use of anecdotes — on gestures and stance	❏ I have checked my speech for length of sentences and awkward words or phrasing. ❏ I have checked that the ideas flow logically. ❏ I have identified any sections where I might lose the audience, and cut or rewritten them. ❏ I have checked that my voice sounds natural, and is not too high, too fast or too slow. ❏ I have checked timing—rate of breathing and delivery of humorous or dramatic lines. ❏ I have identified and worked on removing any annoying habits or habitual gestures. ❏ I have worked on using effective hand gestures.

Sample practice log

DATE	TIME			CONCENTRATE ON	COMMENTS
	ON	OFF	TOTAL		

Step 6: monitor your progress

AREA FOR IMPROVEMENT	ACTION
Monitor your improvement	❑ I have taped 1 2 3 4 5 6 speeches and made notes on what I need to change. ❑ I have sought feedback from others on 1 2 3 4 5 6 occasions. ❑ I have pushed myself to seek greater challenges by: _____

Step 7: become a mentor

AREA FOR IMPROVEMENT	ACTION
Become a mentor	❑ I have agreed to help one or two beginning speakers develop their skills. ❑ I have volunteered to train people in my place of work in public speaking skills.

SOME FINAL HANDY HINTS

Finally, to help you on your road to becoming the 'best speaker in town', here are some handy hints.

Learn to skim-read

This is one of the handiest skills you can develop. You know the easiest way to practise? Find a couple of children who love to have stories read to them. (THAT shouldn't be too hard—there are always your own children, friends' children, grandchildren, neighbours' children.) Pick up the book. Now practise the skill of taking in a sentence or two at a time with one sweep of your eyes and telling the story instead of reading it word-by-word. Use facial expressions; vary your voice levels and accents—go on, be a ham! This audience won't be too critical.

If there are no children handy, practise by reading newspaper articles to your partner or friends. Try to read as naturally as possible, barely glancing at the text on the page.

You'll learn lots of valuable things about dramatisation, using words and holding audience attention. Later, when you need to skim-read those notes in front of you to maintain eye-contact with the audience, your practice sessions will pay off.

Print your notes/key words in lower case

In countless books about public speaking, people will advise you to print key phrases or words in capital letters. Some say to type your whole speech in capitals. The reasoning is, I suppose, that capitals are easier to read at a distance, or stand out more.

For most readers, writing in capital letters actually decreases readability. Any teacher of reading knows this. So to make your notes more readable at a glance, print them:

larger than usual

BUT NOT IN CAPITALS.

Test microphones before you speak

Microphones can be a great asset or a pain in the neck. If you're going to be stuck with one that whines or echoes, you're better off without it. Ditto for the one that is either somewhere near your navel and impossible to adjust, or towering over you so you have to stand on tiptoe and speak up to it like a child begging for a sweet.

If possible, get to the venue early enough to test and, if necessary, adjust the microphones. Work on developing your voice projection so if the room is small enough, you can choose to do without a microphone.

Use props to save the day

You will, no doubt, come across books on public speaking that tell you not to use props, just as they will tell you not to read from a script. Sometimes, however, props will give you the confidence to get through a presentation. My feelings about props? If you really feel you need them, use them.

'Props' can be anything from hand-held cards to physical objects that you will use to illustrate a point. The most important thing is to make sure you remain in control—don't let the props either distract from you as a speaker or ruin your speech if they fail. Let's look at a few different props that you may use:

Hand-held cards

In my early days as a public speaker, I decided to cut cardboard into cards so small they would fit into the palm of my hand. That way, I reasoned, the audience wouldn't even have to know I was using a prop.

During my practice runs everything worked perfectly. I simply opened the palm of my hand, glanced at the words on the card and continued speaking. But nerves do funny things, and at the actual event I found that my hand clenched so tightly on the cards they curled up into nothing.

I didn't let that stop me. In my ongoing quest to be a fearless public speaker, I moved to bigger cards. Everybody could see these, of course, but I'd stopped worrying about that. I printed large key words on them and away I would go. This worked very well for some months until one fateful day when I was speaking in front of 100 people, I found myself saying, three minutes into the address, 'and in conclusion...' Yes, I had forgotten to check the order of the cards.

Goodbye to hand-held cards. Instead, I went the opposite way—I moved sheets of cardboard with the main points on them onto an easel! I had these professionally prepared, and for an information meeting they worked very well. The main problem was transportation.

I finally gave up on these when I took them to Melbourne in a huge suitcase. My fellow traveller, an international speaker from America, looked curiously at the suitcase and asked what was in it.

'The props for my speech,' I told him.

'What happens if they don't arrive?' he asked.

'I don't speak,' I said. At the look of disbelief on his face, I said: 'Well, where are your props?'

'In my head,' he replied. 'Doug, you have to learn to trust your memory.'

At that stage, I felt I still needed some sort of aid—but neither cards nor sheets of paper seemed appropriate. I thought about it for a while and came up with the spiral notebook.

This 'reporter style' notepad, measuring about 12 centimetres x 20 centimetres, can be purchased from any newsagency. The spiral at the top keeps the pages in order, the notebook is small enough not to be a distraction to the audience, and you can print key words on it clearly. You can also turn the pages without anyone realising what you are doing. If you want, you can tape it at the bottom to form the letter 'A' and place it on the table near where you are speaking. If you are working with a large group, place the notebook flat on the lectern, to the left of you.

Now key word your speech with super large letters that you can read from at least 1 metre away.

If you are caught on the hop you can print key words on a napkin, on a drink coaster, or even on the back of a business card or two. The idea is simply to write down those key words that will help you to structure your speech so it makes sense. Unless you have chosen to work from a script, use whatever method works for you to stimulate your memory—just make sure the key words are large enough to read from a distance.

Physical props

Some speakers remind themselves of what they were going to say by setting a variety of objects on a nearby table and using each one as a stimulus for the next point. They must, of course, be relevant to the speech! For example, if you were going to talk about customer service, you could bring with you a telephone, a clock, a large picture of a smiling face, and a box wrapped to look like a gift. Holding up each in turn to focus the attention of the audience on the points you wish to make, you could talk about telephone manner, prompt service, the importance of smiling and a cheerful attitude, and 'added value' of surprise gifts.

These physical props are the equivalent of key words—but if you are travelling some distance to give your speech, such props might take up too much space.

Try a speech in stereo

Once I was invited to do one of those social speeches that everyone hates and agonises over:

What can I say for five minutes?

After thinking about it I had a brainwave—and came up with a way out that I still use to this day. I rang up five other people and invited them to speak for a minute and called the speech 'A Speech In Stereo'. I started it off, said my bit in about 30 seconds and then called on the others to say a few snappy words. Worked like a charm. And the audience liked it, too.

Test any electronic devices

If you are using electronic toys, make sure you check them before you start. As I say in my book *How to Create and Deliver a Dynamic Presentation*:

You're on before you're on.

The three golden rules for *all* props apply particularly to electronic devices:

1. They must not distract from your speech.
2. They should be easy to use and read.
3. They should enhance your speech, not be a part of it.

So when you are thinking of what to do and how to do it, keep these rules in mind.

Tips on audio-visual aids

Remember:

★ If you use an *overhead projector*, try to make sure that it's conveniently placed so nobody has to peer around the machine to see the screen. The screen should be high; the visuals should be large and clear. How clear? Throw your OHP transparency on the floor. If you can't read it while standing above it, it's too small.

★ Similarly, the writing on *flip charts* should be large and clear, without the writing running downhill. Insert a spare piece of paper between the pages to prevent the ink from fibre-tip pens soaking into the next page. Make sure you can anchor the chart firmly; there's nothing more annoying than watching a speaker continually diving to rescue a falling flip chart.

★ *Show-and-tell* is a great way to illustrate a point, but make sure that anything with moving parts will do what it's supposed to do; that you don't end up carrying a huge box full of heavy teaching aids; that you don't 'lose' the audience by continually disappearing from sight to retrieve some other wondrous object; and that the audience doesn't get so interested in what you have to show them that they stop listening to what you have to say.

Measure your impact as a speaker

You will improve dramatically as a speaker if you get into the habit of assessing your effectiveness each time you speak. I don't mean you should sit down afterwards with a notepad and scribble furiously about the guy in the second row who rolled his eyes at every second thing you said, or go home and moan to your family about how gosh-awful you were.

I mean be alert for feedback from the audience at all times. Note small signs that tell you what *impact* you are having on the people listening to you. To measure your impact on your audience, you need only sharpen your observation skills.

Pretend for a moment that while you are watching a speaker, your ears are solidly plugged with cotton wool. You can see everything that is happening in the room—but you can't hear a word the speaker is saying.

How can you possibly assess the speaker's impact? It's easy.

You'll find that the audience acts as that speaker's mirror. It will be looking directly at the speaker, and is likely to be reflecting the emotions they project. It should laugh with them, and cry with them. (Oh well, you can't win them all.)

When you watch for the audience's reaction, you might see some frowns or some heads shaking in disagreement. But at least that means they are awake and listening. Even accomplished speakers don't expect that every member of the audience will like and agree with them; they just don't want to be ignored.

The audience will send you clear signals if you have been effective. Once you become adept at reading those signals, you won't need applause to tell you that you're a hit. You'll know because your listeners have been:

Silent

Attentive

Responsive

So: look around the room as you speak. Establish eye contact with your audience. Look for signals. Are there:

★ biros clicking
★ feet shuffling
★ chairs moving
★ people leaving the room
★ people whispering?

If the answer to any of these questions is 'yes', you aren't off to a very auspicious start. You haven't managed to engage the interest of the group.

But if they are *silent*, you can take heart. That's a good sign. But take a closer look, to make sure they're silent because they're listening, not because they're comatose with boredom or have had too much to eat at lunch.

Observe carefully. Are your listeners maintaining eye contact with you? Are people responding to what you say? Are they nodding in agreement, or shaking their heads angrily? Are they alert, interested and waiting with absorbed attention for your next word?

If you have a silent, attentive and responsive audience you can be sure that you are having a positive impact. You are succeeding as a speaker. You will be almost able to hear the group saying:

Yes! That's what I think, too.

Or:

I didn't know that could happen.

When this happens your message has reached the mind of your listeners.

By closely monitoring audience response every time you speak, by interpreting and acting upon the signals you pick up, you will considerably speed the development of your skills.

PUBLIC SPEAKING: SOMETHING WE DO EVERY DAY OF OUR LIVES

Throughout *How to be the Best Speaker in Town* I have emphasised the development of you as a person in every facet of your life. To relate to others, you first have to value yourself and the contribution you have to make to the world. A warm personality and a positive self-image are wonderful things to possess, but they have to grow out of the real you; they are not something that can be put on like evening clothes.

Your public speaking personality likewise grows out of your experiences and interactions with the world around you. Spoken language cannot be separated from the people who use it. What you say reflects what you believe. What you choose to do with language reveals what type of person you are.

This means that when you set out to become a better speaker you will not only be developing a skill, but you will be involved in a process that is likely to change your personality and transform the quality of your relationships with other people. So it is important that you should make your real aim *self-improvement*. You should not be seeking to improve your speaking skills in order to *manipulate* other people. Your sharing of ideas, and your caring for other people, will be at the heart of personal improvement.

Sensitive interaction at all levels—in private conversations, in groups or in formal speaking situations—will not only help you to achieve your personal goals, it will lead you to greater satisfaction with your everyday life. At the end of it all, you should be able to look at yourself and discover not just a more effective speaker, but a more effective person. What greater reward could be *offered*?

So don't just speak.

COMMUNICATE.

IN SUMMARY...

Your Self-Improvement Program should focus on the following steps:

* Practise the basics of effective public speaking in everyday conversation. Use colourful, expressive language; use strong verbs; make a conscious effort to entertain family and friends; study sitcoms to learn about timing.
* Learn to 'read' other people's reactions to your speeches/conversational gambits.
* In the beginning stages of public speaking, seek out opportunities for making short speeches or presentations.
* Join public speaking clubs or attend public speaking courses.
* Concentrate on speaking on topics that *interest* you. You don't have to be all things to all people.
* Start and maintain a speech file.
* Research your audience every time you speak.
* Practise the basics of writing an effective speech or script.
* Rehearse and practise diligently to attain a polished delivery.
* Get feedback—from a tape, from others.
* Take care of your voice.
* As you deliver more speeches, fine-tune your technique by monitoring your progress.
* Pass your knowledge and skills on to others—become a mentor.

And, finally, remember these handy hints:

* Learn to skim-read and speak sentences rather than 'read them out'.
* Print your notes/keywords in lower case.
* Test microphones in advance.
* Have a variety of props ready for use if they enhance your delivery, but make sure that:
  — they all work
  — you know how to work them.
* Monitor the audience constantly to assess your impact on them.
* Don't just speak: COMMUNICATE!

RECOMMENDED READING

Alessandra, Tony & O'Connor, J. (1990) *People Smart*, Keynote Publishing Co., La Jolla, California.

Bolton, Robert (1986) *People Skills*, Prentice-Hall, Sydney.

Malouf, Doug (1988) *How to Create and Deliver a Dynamic Presentation*, Simon & Schuster, Sydney.

Malouf, Doug (1993) *Switch on Your Magnetic Personality*, RIAL Marketing and Publishing, Deakin, Canberra.

Malouf, Doug (1994) *How To Teach Adults in a Fun and Exciting Way*, Business & Professional Publishing, Sydney.

McInnes, Lisa, Johnson, Daniel & Marsh, Winston (1989) *How To Motivate, Manage and Market Yourself*, co-published by Winston Marsh Pty Ltd, Melbourne, and Daniel Johnson Presentations, Melbourne.

Van Ekeran, Glenn (1994) *Speaker's Sourcebook II*, Prentice-Hall, Englewood Cliffs, New Jersey.

Walters, Lilly (1993) *Secrets of Successful Speakers*, McGraw Hill, New York.

Walters, Lilly (1995) *What To Say When You're Dying On The Platform*, McGraw Hill, New York.

Williams, Linda Verlee (1983) *Teaching for the Two-Sided Mind*, Prentice-Hall, Englewood Cliffs, New Jersey.

INDEX

A
ABC formula, 58–9
anecdotes, 83
apologising, 71
'armchair' talk, 43
attitudes to public speaking, 33–4
audience
   assessment of, 46–8, 120–1, 137
   interaction with, 8
   misjudging, 120
   overloading, 122–3
   reactions, 8
   relevance of speech to, 59–60, 137
audio-visual aids, 148
Australian voice profile, 100–1
auto-suggestion, 28
AVIS, 6

B
Balos, Rowena, 98
BIN, 40
body control, 91
body language, 126, 127, 139
breath support, 101–2

C
cards, hand-held, 145–6
communication, *see also* Verbal communication
   exercise, 9–10
computer technology, 83
confidence, *see* Self-confidence

D
dead space, 89
deep breathing, 28–9

E
embarrassment, 31
enthusiasm, lack of, 125–6
equipment testing, 144–5, 147, 148
ERS technique, 60–2, 66
eye contact, 75–6, 124

F
fear of public speaking, 19, 24–5, 32–3

G
Griffin, Craig, 13

H
humour, 64–5, 83

I
ideas, 54, 82
information overload, 122–3
'information' speeches, 38, 42–4
instructional speech, 43
International Training in Communication (ITC), 135
introductions, 40–1

J
jargon, 123–4

L
language, 2, 133
lectures, 42
left brain, 21
listeners, engaging, 3
listening skills, 134
Lough, John, 44

M
Marsh, Winston, 59
McFarlane, Ken, 120
mental pictures, 109, 114–15
   exercises, 115–17
mentoring, 139
metronome, 125
microphones, 144–5
mirroring technique, 135
model speeches, 81–2
monitoring speeches, 91–2, 139, 149–50
'motivational' speeches, 38, 45–6
movies, aids to speeches, 84

N
natural speaker syndrome, 26–7
nervousness, 24–5
   controlling, 27–30
notes, 31, 144

P
pacing speeches, 125
personal stories, 74
personal styles, assessing, 134–5
pitch, 102
places to practise, 94–5

Index

planning
   checklist, 66
   importance of, 37
   stages, 54–64, 128–30
practising speeches, 20, 22, 88–97, 121, 133
   body control, 91
   checklist, 96–7
   on others, 95
   recording, 91–2
   sessions, 90
   speaking to empty space, 89
   venues, 92–4
preparation, poor, 119
presentation skills, 126–7
props, 145, 146–7
public speaking
   attitudes to, 33–4
   bad practices, 20–1
   clubs, 135
   communication skills for, 7–8
   courses, 135
   fear of, 19, 24–5, 32–3
   impact on self-confidence, 15–16
   myths, 25–32
   problems and solutions, 119–28

R
reading scripts, 70
rehearsing, *see* Practising speeches
relaxation, 28
relevance of speech, 59–60, 137
research, 119–20
right brain, 21–2

S
scripts, 68–77, 137
   checking, 76
   checklist for producing, 69
   disadvantages of, 31
   natural sounding, 74–5
   reading, 70
   samples, 72–3
   typeface, 71–2
self-confidence, 2, 4
   development of, 10, 19, 29
   impact of public speaking skills, 15–16
self-expression, 3
self-image improvement exercises, 17–19
self-improvement, 10, 150–1
   progress log, 140–3
   steps, 132–9
Shaw, George Bernard, 95
signposting, 63
skim-reading, 143
sound, *see* Voice
speakers
   famous, 14–15
   natural, 26–7

speaking, *see also* Public speaking
   effective, 3, 6, 8, 9
   opportunities, 136
speech, power of, 1–2
speeches
   aids, 84
   appropriate to speaker, 48–50
   checklist, 66
   colour coding, 80–1
   delivery, 137–9
   filing, 78–9, 80, 82, 85–6, 136
   information sources for, 79
   models, 81
   practising, 20, 22, 88–97, 121, 133
   purpose of, 38
   structuring, 53–67
   types of, 38–46, 147
   writing, 66, 137
speed of delivery, 124–5
storytelling
   characteristics of good, 114–15
   example, 109–13
   exercises, 115–17
   technique, 112–13
STYLE, 11

T
'thanks' speeches, 38, 39–42
timing, 70, 122, 134, 138
Toastmasters, 30, 135
toasts, 39
tone, 103
topics, choice of, 136

V
Van den Berg, Rebekah, 98
venue practise, 92–4
verbal communication, 3
verbal habits, distracting, 126, 128
voice
   Australian, 100–1
   exercises, 103–7, 138
   good, 100–1
   health, 102
   training, 99
votes of thanks, 41–2

W
warm-up stage, 54, 55–9
word perfect technique, 31
word power, 2
words, 2, 138
wrap-up stage, 63–4
writing
   scripts, 68–77, 137
   speeches, 66

Doug Malouf seminars and products travel the world

Doug can be contacted at:

DTS International
First Floor
6 Flinders Street
North Wollongong NSW 2500 AUSTRALIA

Dial us today for more information:

Phone: (042) 29 8244   Fax: (042) 27 2545

International dialling: Phone: 61 42 29 8244
                            Fax: 61 42 27 2545

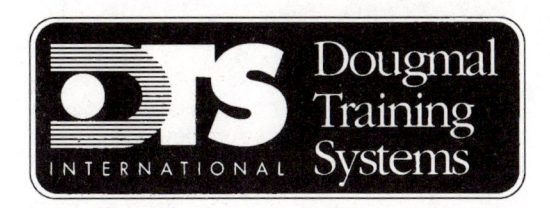

DTS INTERNATIONAL — Dougmal Training Systems